PRAY

St. GERTRUDE

AND

St. MECHTILDE

OF THE ORDER OF

St. BENEDICT

By: St. Gertrude & St. Mechtilde

Imprimatur:

EDM. CAN. SURMONT

Vic. Gen.

Westmonasterii die 16 Augusti 1917

PRAYER TO THE SAINT WHOSE MEMORY THE CHURCH CELEBRATES

I VENERATE and greet thee, O most blessed N., in the sweetest Heart of Jesus Christ, and I congratulate thee with all my heart on that honour wherewith thou wast honoured by God and by all the court of Heaven on this the day of thine entrance therein. And for the increase of thy joy and thy glory I offer thee that same transcendently precious and worthy Heart of Jesus Christ, beseeching thee that thou wouldst deign to pray to God for me, and to assist me in the hour of my death. Amen.

TABLE OF CONTENTS

PART I

DAILY DEVOTIONS

PART II

THE HOLY SACRIFICE OF THE MASS

PART III

THE MOST HOLY TRINITY

TABLE OF CONTENTS

PART IV

PRAYERS TO JESUS CHRIST

PART V

THE PASSION OF OUR LORD

TABLE OF CONTENTS

PART VI

THE BLESSED VIRGIN MARY

PART VII

THE SAINTS

PART VIII

FOR DIFFERENT NECESSITIES

TABLE OF CONTENTS

PART IX

PRAYERS FOR FORGIVENESS

PART X

HOLY COMMUNION

TABLE OF CONTENTS

ADDITIONAL PRAYERS

THIS LITTLE BOOK IS A TRANSLA-
TION, the only one from the Latin, of
the *Preces Gertrudianae,* a manual of
devotions compiled in the seventeenth
century from the *Suggestions of Divine
Piety* of St. Gertrude and St. Mechtilde,
nuns of the Order of St. Benedict. Of
this work Alban Butler says, in his life
of St. Gertrude, that it is " perhaps the
most useful production, next to the writ-
ings of St. Teresa, with which any fe-
male saint ever enriched the Church."
Care has been taken to preserve, not
only the substance, but, as far as might
be, the form, of the original prayers; and
a few others, well known and much
valued, have been added as an Appendix.

Prayers of St. Gertrude and St. Mechtilde

PART I

PRAYERS FOR DAILY USE

MORNING PRAYERS

Our Divine Lord said to St. Mechtilde: When you awake in the morning, let your first act be to salute my Heart, and to offer me your own.

I ADORE, praise, and salute thee, O most sweet Heart of Jesus Christ, fresh and gladdening as the breath of spring, from which, as from a fountain of graces, sweeter than the honeycomb, floweth evermore all good and all delight. I thank thee with all the powers of my heart for having preserved me throughout this night, and for having rendered to God the Father praises and thanksgivings in my behalf. And now, O my sweet Love, I offer thee my wretched and worthless heart as a morning sacrifice; I place it in thy most tender Heart, and entrust it to thy keeping; beseeching thee that thou wouldst deign to pour into it thy divine inspirations, and to enkindle it with thy holy love. Amen.

2 PRAYERS FOR DAILY USE

RECOMMENDATION TO JESUS

It was revealed to St. Gertrude that if any one commends himself to God, praying to be kept from all sin, God will never forsake him; and even though he be permitted to fall into some grievous fault, the grace of God will sustain him like a staff, and enable him to return more easily to repentance.

O JESUS, full of compassion, I commend to thee my spirit and my soul, in union with that love wherewith thou didst commend thine own to the Father on the cross; and I place them in the most sacred wound of thy tender Heart, that they may be therein protected from all the snares of the enemy. Thou knowest, O good Jesus, and I know by my own sad experience, how weak and frail I am, so that I could not of myself persevere in good, or resist temptation even for one single hour. Wherefore I pray thee, by the reverence due to that union wherein thy manhood is united to the adorable Trinity in order to our glorification, that thou wouldst deign to unite my will to thine, and so to strengthen and secure it, that it may be unable to rebel against thee. In union with thy most sinless limbs, I commend to thee all the members of my body, with all their movements, that they may throughout this day move for thy glory alone, for thy praise and thy love. Amen.

ASPIRATION TO JESUS

Jesus said to St. Mechtilde: Whoever shall breathe a sigh towards me from the bottom of his heart when he awakes in the morning, and shall ask me to work all his works in him throughout the day, he will draw me to him; so that his soul shall have life from me even as his body has life from his soul, and he shall do all things through me and by me. For never does a man breathe a sigh of longing aspiration towards me without drawing me nearer to him than I was before.

O MOST loving Jesus, I breathe towards thee this sigh, drawn from the depth of my heart, beseeching thee with all my might that thou wouldst deign thyself to work in me all my works, whether of body or of soul, to cleanse them all in thy sweetest Heart, and to offer them, in union with thine own most perfect works, to God the Father as an eternal thanksgiving. Amen.

INTENTION TO BE FORMED IN THE MORNING

Our Lord revealed to St. Gertrude, that he records with letters of gold in the book of life all those actions which are done purely for the love of God, in union with the Passion of Christ, and for the salvation of all mankind, without thought of our own merit. And although all good works receive from God an abundant reward, those which are done simply and purely for his glory are of far higher merit, and obtain for us a far greater increase of glory.

O LORD, my God, for thy sake I resolve to perform all my actions, whether outward or inward, purely for thy glory, and for the salvation of the whole world; with such intention and in such manner as thou dost desire and enjoin; and in union with that love whereby thy Son came down from heaven, and wrought out the whole work of our salvation, especially during his Passion. Wherefore I entirely disclaim all merit, all reward and grace which I might otherwise hope to obtain by these actions, that I may offer to thee, my God, a pure sacrifice of praise, and give thee a proof of my love.

COVENANT WITH GOD

O ALMIGHTY God, I sanctify, dedicate, and consecrate to thee every beating of my heart, and every pulsation of my blood; and I desire to make this compact with Thee, that their every beating shall say to Thee: Holy, holy, holy, Lord God of Sabaoth; and I beseech thee to impute this meaning to them, so that they may be before thy Divine Majesty as the unceasing echo of that heavenly canticle, which seraphims sing without ceasing unto thee. Amen. Amen.

A MORE EXTENDED COVENANT, TO BE RENEWED
EVERY WEEK

The great efficacy of this covenant may be shown thus: Were a person to resolve that by every movement he made he wished to be understood to ratify and approve all the sins that are committed all over the earth, and to be held a partaker of them, it is easy to see what guilt he would thus contract. And if such an intention would have so great influence for evil, why should it not have immense force and merit for good?

O LORD God, my Creator, all my desire is before thee, and my groaning is not hidden from thee; but inasmuch as the necessities of this life prevent the constant application of my mind to thy praise, I make with thee this covenant, earnestly desiring that it may remain in force throughout this week.

Whenever I look up towards heaven, I desire and intend to rejoice with thee in thine infinite perfections; that thou art what thou art, supremely strong and wise and loving and just.

As often as I open or close my eyes, I desire and intend to approve and concur in all the holy actions which thine only-begotten Son, and all the saints in heaven and just on earth, have ever done, or shall ever hereafter do, to thy glory, and desire to be held a partaker in them all.

As often as I draw my breath, I offer to thee the Life and Passion and Blood of our Lord

Jesus Christ. and the merits and sufferings of all the saints, to thine eternal glory, for the welfare and peace of all the whole world, and in satisfaction for the sins of all men.

Whenever I sigh, I intend to detest and abhor every sin, as well my own sins as those which have ever been committed from the beginning of the world against the honour of thy Name. Would that the slight and worthless offering of my blood might be accepted in satisfaction for them!

Lastly, as often as I move my hand or my foot, so often do I cast myself with entire resignation upon thy most holy will, desiring that thou wouldst dispose of me in time and in eternity, according to thine adorable good pleasure.

And, lest this fivefold covenant should be in any way made void, I seal it with the seals of thy five most Sacred Wounds, earnestly desiring that it may have its full force with thee, even though in any one of these actions it be not actually present to my mind.

ASPIRATION BEFORE PRAYER

Our Lord directed St. Mechtilde to say the following prayer whenever she went into choir, or said the divine office or other prayer; assuring her that she might securely rely on the mercy of God that no prayer thus begun should fail of its effect.

O MOST Holy Father, in union with the love of thy well-beloved Son, I commend my spirit to thee.

PRAYER BEFORE THE DIVINE OFFICE OR

OTHER PRAYER

O ALMIGHTY, everlasting God, I, thy most unworthy creature, appear here before the throne of thy grace, desiring to pour out my heart before thee, and to worship thee, my God, as well and as perfectly as I can. Wherefore I begin and will faithfully continue this divine office [or, this prayer] in union with the love wherewith thy Son worshipped thee, and wrought all the whole work of our redemption; beseeching thee that I may be enabled to pay thee a tribute of honour and praise like that which the most precious Humanity of Jesus and the most holy Virgin Mary rendered thee unceasingly. And to this end I offer these my prayers to thee, in the virtue and merit of the Sacred Heart of Jesus, in his Name and in that of all thy holy angels and saints, to thy eternal praise and glory. I humbly implore thee to preserve me from all distraction and dryness of spirit, and to enable me duly to bring thee this my appointed tribute of prayer and praise. Amen.

ASPIRATION BEFORE THE DIVINE OFFICE

Our Lord recommended St. Mechtilde to say the following brief prayer before reciting her office, promising her that the prayer of those who habitually did so should be united with his own most perfect and availing prayers, and so have an infinite worth before God.

O LORD Jesus, in union with the intention and love with which thou didst give praise to God the Father, I offer and will recite this holy office.

REMEDY AGAINST DISTRACTIONS

When you are distracted in prayer, commend it to the Heart of Jesus, to be perfected by him, as our Lord himself taught St. Gertrude. One day, when she was much distracted in prayer, he appeared to her, and held forth to her his Heart with his own sacred hands, saying: Behold, I set my Heart before the eyes of thy soul, that thou mayest commend to it all thine actions, confidently trusting that all that thou canst not of thyself supply to them will be therein supplied, so that they may appear perfect and spotless in my sight.

Remember always to say the Gloria Patri with great devotion. The hermit Honorius relates that a certain monk who had been accustomed to say his office negligently appeared to another after his death and being asked

*what sufferings he had to undergo in punish-
ment of his carelessness, he said that all had
been satisfied for and effaced by the reverent
devotion with which he had always said the*
Gloria Patri.

ASPIRATION AFTER THE DIVINE OFFICE

*While St. Mechtilde was praying for one who
had complained to her that she frequently said
her hours with great distractions, she received
this answer from our Lord: Let her always say,
after each hour, the following prayer; adding,
that if it could not be said punctually after
each separate hour, it should at least be said
seven times during the day.*

O GOD, be merciful to me a sinner! *or*, O
most meek and gentle Lamb of God, have
mercy on me, and deign to supply all my defects and negligences in saying this hour.

PRAYER AFTER OFFICE, OR ANY OTHER PRAYER

O LORD Jesus, I commend this my lukewarm and distracted service to thy Divine
Heart, that it may be therein cleansed and perfected; I offer it to thee in union with the love
with which thou didst endure death, and set
forth thy death, together with all the fruit of
thy holy Incarnation, before God the Father
on the day of thine ascension.

AN EFFICACIOUS METHOD OF OFFERING OUR

ACTIONS TO GOD

While St. Gertrude was offering a certain action to God, saying:

O Lord, I offer thee this work through thine only Son, in the power of the Holy Spirit, to the praise of thy eternal Majesty; *it was revealed to her that whatever action was thus offered would acquire a worth and acceptableness to God beyond all human comprehension. For as all things appear to be green when seen through a green glass, so whatever is offered to God through his only-begotten Son cannot be otherwise than most precious and pleasing in his sight.*

That you may understand how useful it is to offer all your works to God, listen to what our Lord said on one occasion to St. Gertrude: All thy works are most perfectly pleasing to me. And as she could not believe this, he added: If you held in your hand some object which you had the means and the skill to render perfectly pleasing to every one, and if you tenderly loved that object, would you neglect to adorn it?   Even thus, because you are accustomed to offer all your works to me, I hold them in my hand; and as I have both the power and the skill, my love rejoiceth to cleanse and perfect them all, that they may be most perfectly pleasing in my sight.

PRAYER ON LEAVING CHURCH

O MOST pitiful Jesus, I give thee thanks for every good gift which thou hast bestowed on me in this church. And now that I am about to leave it, I offer thee, in union with thy own most perfect prayers, all the prayers and other devotions which I have performed therein; beseeching thee that thou wouldst deign to ennoble and perfect them in thy Divine Heart, to unite them with every holy intention and every feeling of devotion which thou hast ever elicited from any heart of man, and to offer them to God the Father, for all my negligences and omissions, as a grateful satisfaction and a most acceptable sacrifice; and I implore thee to grant me that most holy blessing which thou gavest to thine apostles when thou didst ascend into heaven, so that by its force and efficacy I may be enabled to persevere in thy grace, and to serve thee faithfully evermore. Amen.

AT TAKING HOLY WATER

BY the sprinkling of thy Precious Blood, O Lord Jesus Christ, and by the merit of thy Passion, wash me from every stain, and cleanse me from all sin. In the Name of the Father, etc.

HOW PLEASING IT IS TO OUR LORD TO PRAY WITH HANDS OUTSTRETCHED IN FORM OF THE CROSS

St. Gertrude said to our Lord: Teach me, O thou best Teacher, some one way at least in which we may most specially set forth the memory of thy holy Passion. Our Lord answered her thus: When you pray, spread forth your hands so as to represent to God the Father the memory of my Passion, in union with that love with which I stretched out my hands on the cross; and if you do this habitually, without fear of ridicule or reproach, you will pay me an honour as great as is shown to a king when he is solemnly enthroned.

WHEN THE CLOCK STRIKES

O MOST sweet Jesus, I commend to thy Divine Heart all that I have done in the hour that is gone, to be cleansed and purified, and offered to God the Father for his eternal praise. And whatsoever I shall do in the hour that is beginning, I resolve to do simply and purely for the glory of God and for the salvation of all mankind, in union with thy Passion. Amen.

BEFORE WORK

Our Lord directed St. Gertrude to tell a certain person to form the following intention before beginning any work:

O LORD Jesus, in union with thy most perfect actions I commend to thee this my work, to be directed according to thy adorable will, for the salvation of all mankind. Amen.

AFTER WORK

O LORD Jesus, in union with thy most perfect actions I offer thee this my work, to be amended and cleansed, and presented as is fit to God the Father, to his eternal praise. Amen.

BEFORE EATING

Our Lord said to St. Gertrude: He who takes care to eat and drink, &c., with the intention expressed in the following prayer, holds as it were a buckler before me, to defend me from the insults and injuries of the worldly.

O LORD Jesus, I take this food in that same love wherewith thou hast sanctified it, when in thy most holy Humanity thou didst deign to eat and to drink to the glory of God the Father, and for the salvation of all the whole human race; beseeching thee that, in union with thy divine love, it may tend to the increase of glory, and salvation of all thine elect in heaven, on earth, or in purgatory.

WHILE EATING

St. Gertrude was accustomed to say frequently while eating:

MAY the virtue of thy divine love incorporate me wholly into thee, O my most loving Jesus!

And while drinking:

O MOST loving Jesus, pour into my heart and preserve within me the energy of thine own most glowing charity; may it pervade all my substance, and flow evermore through every faculty of my body and soul, to thine eternal praise and glory. Amen.

She asked our Lord whether he would accept a like devotion from all who might offer it to him, and received this reply: Whenever any one eats or drinks with this intention and devotion, I will acknowledge in presence of my Father that I have eaten with him, and that he has given me to drink, and I will show to him in due time the utmost tenderness of my love.

AFTER FALLING INTO SIN

St. Gertrude said to our Lord: Teach me, O best of Teachers, how to efface the stains of sin which I contract from time to time. She received this answer: Never allow these stains to remain upon thy conscience; but as soon as thou feelest thyself defiled by any fault, say to me with a devout heart:

O CHRIST Jesus, my only Salvation and Hope, grant that all my transgressions may be blotted out by thy most efficacious death. Amen.

EVENING PRAYERS

A THANKSGIVING OF WONDERFUL EFFICACY

HAIL, my God, Light and Salvation of my soul, may all that is in the round world, and within the circle of the heavens, and in the depths of the abyss, give thee thanks for all the benefits and tender mercies which thou hast bestowed on me in body and in soul. And as the number of them is so great that I cannot answer thee for one of a thousand, I make over this my duty to that eternal, infinite, un-failing gratitude whereby every debt to thee is acquitted by thyself, and through thyself, and in thyself, O thou bright and ever-peaceful Trinity; and obtruding myself on thy notice as a grain of dust, I offer thee, through him who stands at thy right hand in the truth of my substance, such praise and thanksgiving as thou hast enabled us by thy Spirit to render to thee. Amen.

Here examine your conscience, and make an act of contrition, saying with a sigh:

O MOST loving Father, in the bitterness of the Passion of Jesus Christ thy Son I pour forth now my complaint, indignantly accusing myself that I have served thee so unfaithfully this day, and have offended thee, my most kind and loving Father, by so many and so great negligences. I grieve for them all from my inmost heart, and smite my breast in the spirit of true contrition, and say unto thee: God be merciful to me a sinner! And for all the negligences whereby I have ever quenched thy good and gentle Spirit within me, I offer thee the sorrows and the tears of thy beloved Son. I beseech thee, in union with his most availing prayers, to grant me the pardon of my sins, and the supply of all my defects. Deign to hear this my humble prayer through that love which did hold back thine arm from taking vengeance when thy only and most beloved Son, the object of thine eternal and ineffable complacency, was numbered with transgressors. Amen.

Our Lord directed St. Mechtilde to repeat three times a day the psalm, Laudate Dominum, omnes gentes, *in penance for her sins.* (*See p. 205.*)

RECOMMENDATION TO THE SACRED HEART
OF JESUS

O SWEETEST Heart of Jesus, to thee I commend my body and my soul this night, that they may calmly rest in thee. And as I cannot praise my God while I sleep, do thou deign to supply my lack of service, and for every beating of my heart give praise to the most Holy Trinity on my behalf; receive into thyself every breath I draw, and offer them all to God as glowing sparks of divine love. Amen.

TO THE BLESSED VIRGIN, AND OTHER THE SAINTS

TO thy maternal faithfulness and to thy special care, O most blessed Virgin Mary, I commend myself this night, beseeching thee to protect me from all the snares of the enemy. O my beloved angel guardian, and you, holy saints, my patrons, defend me and keep me in safety through this night. Praise my God for me without ceasing while I sleep, and deign to bestow on me your blessing in answer to my humble prayer. Amen.

INTENTION BEFORE SLEEP

Taught to St. Gertrude by our Lord.

O LORD JESUS, I accept this sleep in the love with which thou didst sanctify it when thou didst deign to sleep in thy most sacred Humanity, to the glory of God the Father, and for the salvation of all the whole human race; beseeching thee that, in union with thy divine Love, it may tend to the increase in grace and glory of all thine elect, in heaven, on earth, and in purgatory. Amen.

Before you lie down to sleep, trace on your forehead these four letters, I. N. R. I., *saying:*

MAY Jesus of Nazareth, King of the Jews, preserve me from sudden and unprepared death. Amen.

Our Lord revealed to St. Edmund that those who use this prayer shall be preserved from sudden death in the night.

On one occasion when St. Gertrude could not sleep, she learned this prayer from Christ himself.

BY thine own eternal and unruffled repose in the bosom of God the Father, by thy most peaceful rest in the womb of the Blessed Virgin, by the most ecstatic rapture with which thou didst ever take thy delight in the hearts of those who love thee, I beseech thee, O most loving Lord, deign to grant me needful sleep, not for my pleasure or advantage, but that the weary members of my body may be refreshed to labour for thy eternal praise and glory. Amen.

PART II

FOR THE HOLY SACRIFICE OF THE

MASS

Our Lord said to St. Mechtilde: Receive it as a most certain truth, that if any one hears Mass devoutly and fervently, I will send him, for his consolation and defence in the hour of his death, as many of the glorious spirits who stand around my throne as he shall have heard Masses with devotion. And on another occasion he said: However guilty a man may be, however inveterate the enmity of his heart against me, I will patiently bear with him whenever he is present at Mass, and will readily grant him the pardon of his sins, if he sincerely ask it.

Be ever ready, then, to assist at the Holy Sacrifice of the Mass, and strive to penetrate your soul with the spirit of the prayers which follow; they contain the true method of hearing Mass, and are most availing with God.

PRAYER BEFORE MASS

O ALMIGHTY, everlasting God, seeing that it is the true faith of thy Church that the holy sacrifice of the Mass instituted by thy Son is infinitely pleasing to thy divine Majesty, and renders thee an infinite worship and praise, and since by it alone thou canst be worthily and adequately worshipped and praised; impelled by an ardent desire of thy honour and glory, I purpose to assist at this present sacrifice with the utmost devotion of which I am capable, and to offer this most Holy Oblation to thee in union with thy priest. I offer thee not only this sacrifice, but all those which shall be this day offered up from every part of the world; and I protest before thee that if it depended on me whether they should be offered or omitted, I would put forth all my powers to procure and to further their being offered. And were I able now to raise up to thee, of the stones which are scattered over the earth, most devoted priests, who should day by day and with glowing fervour offer to thee this sacrifice of praise, I would most gladly do it. But, being what I am, I implore thee, O most holy Father, through Jesus Christ thy Son, to pour into the hearts of all thy priests, and especially those who might perchance otherwise offer thee this acceptable sacrifice coldly and without due recollectedness, the spirit of grace and of fervour, that they may be enabled to celebrate thy tremendous Mystery with becoming awe and devotion. Grant to me, and to all those who are here present with me, that we may join in this most sacred action with reverence and devotion, so that we may have our portion in its fruit and effect. I confess to thee, O almighty God, and to the Blessed Mary ever Virgin, and to all the Saints, my own sins and those of all the world; and I lay them on thy sacred Altar, that they may be entirely blotted out by the virtue of this sacrifice. Do thou deign to grant us this grace, by that love which held back thy hand from smiting when thy most beloved Son, thy only Son, was immolated by the hands of ungodly men. Amen.

As the Mass varies day by day, from the Introit to the Offertory, you may vary your prayers according to your devotion. (*See* p. 243.)

AT THE OFFERTORY

O MOST merciful Father, in union with that unimaginable love wherewith thy only Son offered to thee the whole influx of the Godhead into his Humanity, and thus with ineffable gratitude referred it back to its immeasureable, unfathomable source, I offer thee whatever gifts and graces thou hast ever bestowed on me of thy sovereign and unutterable goodness; and I lay them on thine altar, together with the merits and graces of the same thy Son, as a sacrifice of everlasting praise, and a pledge and expression of my boundless gratitude to thee. More especially, I offer thee my heart, all too defiled and loathsome as it is; and I plunge it into this Chalice, to the end and with the desire that all the prayers and benedictions which shall be spoken over this Chalice may be spoken also over my heart, and that by the virtue of the ineffable consecration whereby thou changest this wine into the Blood of thy Son, it may be wholly turned to the perfect and constraining love of thee.

And that I may obtain these my petitions, I unite myself to all the love and the gratitude with which thy Son endured all his sorrows; and I offer to thee whatever sorrow or affliction thy fatherly love has ever laid on me or any son of man in order to our salvation, beseeching thee that they may come up before thee in union with this sacrifice as a sweet-smelling odour, and may avail for our salvation.

Finally, in union with the resignation of thy only Son I offer and resign myself to thy most holy will, beseeching thee with my whole heart that thy adorable good pleasure may always in all things be done in me and by me and in all that concerns me. To this end I lay at thy feet, O thou King of kings and my Lord, all my substance and being, my body and my soul, to serve thee henceforth and evermore to the glory of thy most worshipful Majesty. Amen.

When St. Gertrude had thus offered herself to our Lord on one occasion, he said to her: This offering of thy good will is as it were a royal sceptre in my hand, and a rejoicing and a glory to me in presence of all my angels and saints.

And whenever thou renewest this intention be-
fore me, it is as though that sceptre budded
and put forth most fragrant flowers.

At Orate Fratres, *say with the server:* Sus-
cipiat, &c.

AT THE SECRETA

LOOK down, O tender Father, from the throne of thy Majesty and from the lofty dwelling-place of thy heavens, upon this oblation which our holy Mother the Church, thy Bride, offers to thee by the hands of thy priest; and through its force and merit be appeased for our manifold transgressions. Accept, I beseech thee, the sacrifice which I, thy most worthless servant, offer to thee my living and true God in my own name and in that of all the whole world; in union with all the merits of thy most beloved Son, with all the treasure of thy holy Church, for my innumerable sins, offences, and negligences, and for all the faithful, living and departed, that to them and to me it may avail for salvation unto eternal life. Amen.

AT THE PREFACE

While St. Mechtilde was praying for a certain
person, our Lord said to her: Behold, I pardon
all her sins, in satisfaction for them, while the
priest is reciting these words of the Preface,
Per quem Majestatem, &c., let her praise me in

*union with all my angels and saints, and offer
a* Pater noster *to God through me; thus shall
all her negligences be forgiven and effaced.
And all who shall do this may confidently expect the like blessing at my hands.*

O MOST compassionate Jesus, I adore thee,
I praise and magnify thee in union with
that transcendent praise which the most holy
and worshipful Trinity renders unceasingly to
himself; which flows down thence upon the
most blessed Virgin Mary and upon all Saints
and Angels, who adore thy glorious Majesty
with unceasing and unutterable canticles, and
show forth thy praise in rapturous accord.
With whose voices we beseech thee to permit
ours to blend, saying in lowly acknowledgement: Holy, holy, holy, &c.

Here say as follows a Pater *to supply all your
negligences and defects.*

O MOST holy Father, I offer thee this
prayer in union with the praises with
which heaven and earth and all thy creatures
worship and magnify thee. Deign to hear and
accept it through Jesus Christ thy Son, for all
that is offered to thee through him comes up
before thee well-pleasing and most acceptable.
I beseech thee, through the same thy Son, to
forgive me all my sins and to supply all my
defects and negligences. Amen.

AT THE CANON

O INEFFABLE God, we are now drawing near to those tremendous Mysteries which neither Cherubim nor Seraphim nor all the virtues of heaven suffice to comprehend, for thou alone knowest with what energy of love thou dost daily offer thyself to God the Father upon the altar as a victim of praise and propitiation. And therefore all choirs and orders of Angels adore this thy most sacred and impenetrable secret with lowliest prostration, and behold with awe their King and their Lord, who once came down from heaven in unutterable love to redeem man, now again mysteriously present upon the altar, hidden beneath the mean and lowly species of bread and wine for the salvation of men.

O good Jesus, this work which thou art now about to work is so transcendently adorable that I dare not even look up to thee from the depth of my nothingness. Wherefore I bury myself in the lowest, deepest valley of humiliation I can find, and there await the portion of thy substance that falleth to me, for salvation goeth forth from thee upon all thine elect. Would, O loving Jesus, that my weak arm might aid thee in thy divine work, and obtain for this most holy oblation its full effect according to its ineffable dignity and worth, to effect this the most weary and painful toil would be sweet and light to me. Wherefore I pray thee, grant to this thy priest that he may with due reverence handle thee and offer thee, so that this our oblation may have its fullest force and efficacy on all the living and departed. Amen.

AT THE ELEVATION OF THE HOST

HAIL, sweetest Jesus, prostrate in lowliest humility, I worship and adore thee.

Here strike your breast three times, and say:

O JESUS, have mercy on me!
O good Jesus, spare me!
O most compassionate Jesus, be merciful to me a sinner!

PRAYER TO GOD THE FATHER

O MOST loving Father, in union with that love wherewith thy Son offered himself once upon the cross, and now offers himself to thee upon the altar, I offer him to thee for the welfare and salvation of all thy whole Church. Look upon his virgin Flesh, so cruelly torn by the scourges, bruised with blows and buffetings, defiled with spittings, besmeared with Blood, pierced with sharp thorns, swollen and livid with stripes, torn by the nails, rent with the lance. May that pity which drew him down from heaven and sweetly constrained him to immolate himself on the cross, and constrains him now to offer himself daily to thee upon the altar; may that same pity move thee now, O Father, to have mercy on us. Amen.

AT THE ELEVATION OF THE CHALICE

HAIL, most precious Blood of my Lord, prostrate before thee in lowliest devotion, I worship and adore thee.

Here strike your breast three times, and say:

O SACRED Blood, wash me!
O roseate Blood, cleanse me!
O most precious Blood, cry for me unto God the Father, that he may have mercy on us!

PRAYER AFTER THE ELEVATION, OF GREAT EFFICACY

O MOST holy Father, now that thine only-begotten Son, here truly present upon the altar, has deigned to become a sacrifice and propitiation for our sins, I offer thee his most holy Body and Blood, his Humanity and his Divinity, his virtues and his perfections, his Passion and Death, in union with that love with which he once offered himself to thee upon the cross, and now offers himself to thee on the altar. And in union with these I offer thee the virtues, merits, and graces of the Blessed Virgin Mary and all the Saints, together with all the good works of all men, and all the whole treasure of thy holy Church. And I desire especially to add to these what-

ever of good I and those who are dear to me
have ever done, and whatever afflictions we
have suffered for thy glory. And in union
with this sacrifice, and with all those which are
offered to thee all over the world, I offer to
thee this oblation, O Eternal Father, through
thy beloved Son, in the power of the Holy
Ghost, to thy supreme praise and glory, in
acknowledgement of thy supreme Majesty, and
dominion, and in thanksgiving for all the benefits and the graces thou hast ever bestowed on
any creature, and in full reparation for every
injury or insult ever offered to thee by any
whom thy hands have made.

I offer it to thee for the increase of the joy
and glory of the sacred Humanity of our Lord
Jesus Christ, in worship and veneration of all
the mysteries of his life and death, for the increase of the glory and blessedness of the
Blessed Virgin Mary and of all the Saints, especially my holy Patrons, and those whose
memory we this day celebrate.

Lastly, I offer it to thee on behalf of myself,
a most miserable sinner, and for all my friends,
whether in the order of nature or of grace [es-
pecially N.], and for all Christians living and
departed [especially N.]; beseeching thee that
thou wouldst deign to accept it as an adequate
and sufficient thanksgiving for all the benefits
and graces which thou hast ever bestowed on
our bodies and souls, to impart to us all the
grace needful for us, to turn away from us all

evil of body and of soul which might hinder
our salvation, and to grant us perfect and entire remission of all our sins and negligences.
For all these ends, I offer thee all the love with
which Jesus Christ thy Son our Lord has ever
loved thee, and all the satisfaction he has
made to thee for our sins. Through him and
with him and in him be all honour and glory
unto thee, O God, Father Almighty, in the
unity of the Holy Ghost, for ever and ever.
Amen.

Here say Pater noster *with the priest, and add
the following prayer for the sins of the whole
church. It was revealed to the Saint that this
devotion is most pleasing to God.*

O MOST tender Jesus, I offer to thee this
prayer in union with the most perfect intention with which thou didst sanctify it in
thy Sacred Heart and enjoin it for our salvation; for the forgiveness of all our sins and the
supply of all the defects caused by our frailty,
our ignorance, or our fault, in opposition to
thine irresistible almightiness, thine unsearchable wisdom and thy free and superabounding
goodness. Amen.

AT THE AGNVS DEI

*Beseech our Lord to offer himself to God the
Father as he does in every Mass, according to
the revelation made to St. Gertrude.*

O LAMB of God have mercy on us, and offer thyself to God the Father with all thy humility and all thy patience, in satisfaction for our sins.

O Lamb of God, have mercy on us, and offer thyself to God the Father with all the bitterness of thy Passion, for our reconciliation to God.

O Lamb of God, have mercy on us, and offer thyself to God the Father with all the love of thy divine Heart, for the supply of all our necessities. Amen.

Here you may say part of the prayer which follows the Mass, p. 33.

AT THE DOMINE, NON SVM DIGNVS

O LORD, I am not worthy that the earth should bear me; but for thine own sake pardon me all my sins.

O Lord, I am not worthy to be called thy creature; but by the bitterness of thy passion forgive me all my debts.

O Lord, I am not worthy to utter thy Holy Name; but by the virtue of this holy sacrifice bestow on me thy grace. Amen.

Here make an act of spiritual communion, saying with St. Gertrude and with St. Mechtilde:

O THOU Stream from the Lifegiving Fountain, thou fragrance and sweetness of divine delight, I prostrate myself in my in-

digence and my misery in presence of thine
overflowing fulness. I set before thee my sorrow and my tears, that, by reason of my exceeding unworthiness, my soul must go away
fasting from thine uncloying banquet. And
now, O thou who hast formed my substance
and reformed it when fallen and decayed,
I beseech thee so to prepare me by thine all-
powerful wisdom, and by the tender compassionate love of thy Heart, that I may
worthily receive thee unto my soul, and that
thou mayest work and perfect in me without
impediment all that thou hast from eternity
decreed concerning me, according to the good
pleasure of thy divine will. Amen.

To this end say, if you have time, a Pater
noster, *as our Lord taught St. Mechtilde.*

AT THE COMMUNION

O ALMIGHTY Love, I praise thee; O most
ravishingly sweet Love, I glorify thee; O
most gentle and tender Love, I magnify thee
in and for all the good which thy most glorious
Godhead and thy most blessed Humanity
have ever wrought in us, or shall hereafter
work in us, through that most august and
adorable instrument, thy divine Heart. Amen.

AT THE POST-COMMUNION

BEHOLD, O Heavenly Father, our holy Mother the Church has sent up before thee from thine altar that Victim of transcendent worth whom thou didst send to be immolated for us. Vouchsafe, therefore, to accept it with that ineffable love with which thou didst receive thy Son when he came back from this our far country into thy kingdom, and set forth before thee all the fruit of his sacred Humanity and the glorious wounds of his Flesh. O most compassionate Father, let not his scars depart from before thine eyes for ever, that thou mayest be perpetually put in mind what great and superabounding satisfaction he hath made thee for our sins. Wherefore I beseech thee, in the virtue and efficacy of this unbloody oblation, have mercy on me, and on all sinners, and on all the faithful living and departed; grant unto them grace and mercy, remission of sins, and everlasting life. Amen.

AT THE BLESSING

O GOOD Jesus, may thine omnipotence bless me, may thy wisdom teach me, may thy sweetness fill and pervade me, may thy goodness draw me and unite me to thee for ever. Amen.

At the words,

And the Word was made flesh, and dwelt among us,

bow your head in devout gratitude, and say:

I THANK and bless thee, O good Jesus, that for love of me thou didst deign to be made man. *If any one does this, said our Lord, I will graciously incline my Head towards him in return, and will offer to God the Father all the fruit of my Incarnation, with all the love of my Heart, for the increase of that man's blessedness and glory.*

ACT OF ADORATION OF THE MOST HOLY SACRAMENT

HAIL., most glorious Body and most precious Blood of my Lord Jesus Christ, here truly present beneath these sacramental species; I adore thee with all that devotion and awe wherewith the nine choirs of angels worship and adore thee. I prostrate myself before thee in the spirit of humility, believing and professing that thou, my Lord and my God, are herein most truly contained.

Hail, most glorious Body of Jesus Christ my Saviour, true Victim immolated upon the cross, I adore thee in union with that adoration with which thy Humanity adored thy Godhead, and I give thee thanks with all the love of all thy creatures, that thou dost deign to remain hidden in this tabernacle for our salvation.

Hail, compassionate Jesus, Word of the Father, Brightness of his glory, Ocean of pity, Salvation of the world, most august and sacred

Victim, Hail, Jesus Christ, Splendour of the Father, Prince of Peace, Gate of Heaven, True Bread, Son of the Virgin, Shrine of the Godhead.

I most firmly believe that thou, my God, art here present, and that thou art looking out upon me from behind the veil of the sacrament, and dost behold all the most secret recesses of my heart. I believe that under this species of bread are contained not only thy Flesh and thy Blood, but also thy Divinity and thy Humanity. And although this mystery surpasses my understanding, I nevertheless believe it so firmly that I am ready to give my life and my blood in defence of its truth.

I fall down before thee with most profound reverence, O most Holy Sacrament, and with Angels and Archangels, with Thrones and Dominations, with Cherubim and Seraphim, and with all the glorious array of the heavenly host, I sing to thy glory, saying: Blessed a thousand, yea, ten thousand fold, be the most Holy Sacrament of the Altar!

O thou most intimate and tender Love of the Father's Heart, I give thee thanks, in union with the ineffable mutual thanksgiving and gratitude of the three adorable Persons of the glorious and most worshipful Trinity, that thou hast condescended to institute this priceless Sacrament, by which heaven and earth are made one, and both are unceasingly filled with the infinite treasures of thy grace.

I glorify and magnify thy wise and tender almightiness; I praise and adore thy almighty and gentle wisdom; I bless and praise thine almighty and most wise and gentle love, O Christ Jesus, for that thou hast condescended to devise and hast been strong to institute this ineffably magnificent Sacrament to be the strength and the succour of our salvation.

O Christ Jesus, thou faithful and only Trust of my soul, I praise thee, I love thee, I worship and adore thee; and I humbly implore thee, that as thou didst offer thyself once upon the cross for the sin of the whole world, so thou wouldest now deign to offer thyself to God the Father for my exceeding sins.

O Christ Jesus, my sweetest and my only Love, look with the eyes of thy compassionate mercy on me, a most miserable sinner, here prostrate before thee and imploring with my whole heart the forgiveness of my sins.

O thou princely Flower from the Root of Jesse, by the unutterable love of thy most sweet heart have mercy on me, and receive me into thy favour, for the glory of thy Name.

O most loving Father, I offer to thee this thy beloved Son as a holocaust of unceasing praise, and as a perpetual sacrifice of propitiation for all our sins. Look, I beseech thee, on the face of thy Christ, and remember that most abundant satisfaction which he made to thee for our sins on the cross, and have mercy on us. Amen.

PART III

FIVE HYMNS OF PRAISE TO THE MOST

HOLY TRINITY

AND OTHER DEVOTIONS

These five hymns, taken from the devotions of St. Gertrude, are so sublime and so divine that they seem to be utterances of the Blessed in the heavenly country rather than of pilgrims here on earth. They may be used in solemn processions, or at other times when you feel especially drawn to praise God.

HYMN I

OF THE THREE CHILDREN IN THE FIERY FURNACE

B LESSED art thou, O Lord, the God of our fathers: and worthy to be praised and glorified and exalted above all for ever.

And blessed is the holy Name of thy glory: and exceedingly to be praised, and glorious for ever.

Blessed art thou in the holy temple of thy glory: and exceedingly to be praised, and glorious for ever.

Blessed art thou on the holy throne of thy kingdom: and exceedingly to be praised, &c.

Blessed art thou in the sceptre of thy Godhead: and exceedingly to be praised, &c.

Blessed art thou that sittest above the Cherubim and beholdest the depths: and exceedingly to be praised, &c.

Blessed art thou that walkest on the wings of the wind and on the waves of the sea: and exceedingly to be praised, &c.

Let all thine angels and saints bless thee: praise thee, and glorify thee for ever.

Let heaven and earth, the sea, and all that is in them, bless thee: and let them praise thee, and glorify thee for ever.

Glory be to the Father, and to the Son, and to the Holy Ghost: most blessed and glorious for ever.

Blessed art thou, O Adonai, our Lord, Father of our Lord Jesus Christ, who hast made heaven and earth, and all that is in them: and art blessed and glorious and exalted over all for ever.

HYMN II

IN WHICH THE SAINTS ARE CALLED UPON TO PRAISE GOD

O GOD of my heart, may all the choirs of angels and all the throng of thy saints shout for joy unto thee for me: whom thou hast predestinated from all eternity to thy glory.

May the seven glorious spirits who stand continually before the presence of the throne of thy glory: shout for joy unto thee for me.

May the countless bands of holy angels, whom thou sendest to minister to the elect race whom thou hast purchased to thyself: shout for joy unto thee for me.

May the four-and-twenty ancients, with all the patriarchs and prophets, who fall down before thee and cast their crowns before thy throne: shout for joy unto thee for me.

May the four living creatures having wings, which day and night show forth thy praise: shout for joy unto thee for me.

May the most loving and worshipful brotherhood of the Apostles, by whose intercessions thou dost wonderfully sustain thy Church: shout for joy unto thee for me.

May the victor army of thy martyrs, whose robes are ruddy with thy precious Blood: shout for joy unto thee for me.

May the goodly host of thy confessors, whom thou hast translated into thy marvellous light: shout for joy unto thee for me.

May all thy holy and unspotted Virgins, clothed upon with the serene splendour of thy snow-white purity: shout for joy unto thee for me.

May they shout aloud unto thee for me that new song which breaks forth evermore from their hearts as they follow thee whithersoever thou goest: O Jesus, Bridegroom of Virgin souls.

May all the whole army of thine elect, thine own peculiar people, shout for joy unto thee for me: for thou art their God, and they are thy people for ever.

May all thy marvellous works throughout heaven and earth shout for joy unto thee for me: and render back to thee, its source, the glory which streams everlastingly from thee.

Glory be to the Father, and to the Son, and to the Holy Ghost: and glory to the Queen of heaven, with all the multitude of the heavenly hierarchy, for ever. Amen.

HYMN III

IN WHICH GOD IS GLORIFIED IN THE BLESSED VIRGIN

O MY God, may the most Blessed Virgin Mary ever bless thee: whom thou didst deign to predestinate from eternity to be thy Mother.

Let that admirable Tabernacle of thy glory ever praise thee: sole abode on earth meet for thy holy habitation.

Let the glory of thy Godhead bless thee: which condescended to go down into that lowly virginal valley.

Let the inventive wisdom of thy Godhead bless thee: by which thou didst impart to that Virgin Rose so great virtue and comeliness, that thou didst thyself desire her beauty.

Let thine unspeakable goodness bless thee: the abundant grace of which rendered the whole life of Mary worthy of thy dignity.

Let thy tender love bless thee: by the force of which thou, the peerless flower of virginity, didst become the Virgin's Son.

Let the splendour of the countenance of thy glory bless thee: which so adorned the soul of the Virgin that the ineffable Trinity delighted in her.

Let thine incomprehensible wisdom bless thee: which filled the most chaste spirit of the Virgin with knowledge and understanding.

Let thy lowly and adorable condescension bless thee: whereby thou didst deign to suck the breasts of the most chaste Virgin, as the antidote of the poison of our sins.

Let the ravishing sweetness of thy Sacred Heart bless thee: wherewith thou didst inebriate thy Mother's virgin soul with calm, unutterable delights.

Let the most gracious words of thy divine lips bless thee: which enkindled thy Mother's deepest heart with the holy flame of charity.

Let all the virtue of thy Divinity bless thee, and all the substance of thy Humanity: which deigned to pour into the heart of Mary the whole fulness of heavenly gifts.

Glory be to the Father, and to the Son, and to the Holy Ghost: and glory to the Queen of heaven, with all the multitude of the heavenly hierarchy, for ever. Amen.

HYMN IV

IN WHICH THE HUMANITY OF JESUS IS INVOKED TO PRAISE GOD FOR US

O SWEETEST Jesus, let thine emptying thyself of thy Majesty bless thee for me: which obtained for us the priceless treasure of everlasting glory.

Let thine assumption of our humanity bless thee: whereby thou hast called us to be partakers of the Divine nature.

Let the weary exile thou didst endure for three-and-thirty years bless thee: whereby thou hast brought back to eternal life the souls that had perished.

Let all the anguish and grief of thy Humanity bless thee: by which thou hast sanctified all our afflictions and our toil.

Let thine experience of our misery bless thee: whereby thou hast become unto us the Father of exceeding compassion.

Let all the drops of thy most precious Blood bless thee: by which thou hast cleansed us from the stains of our sins.

Let thy five most precious Wounds, thy most radiant adornment, bless thee: by which thou hast purchased for us mansions in the everlasting inheritance.

Let the bitterness of thy sacred death bless thee: in which thy love, stronger than death, bowed thy Head for us.

Let the excessive sweetness of thy deified heart bless thee: which broke on the cross with impetuous love and grief.

Let the most undefiled flesh of thy Humanity bless thee: in which thou wast made unto us a brother most loving and constant.

Let thy triumphant glory bless thee for me: whereby thou sittest at the right hand of the Father in our flesh for ever.

Let thine own dazzling radiance, thy honour and thy might, bless thee for me: wherewith all the heavenly host is wondrously filled and fed evermore.

Glory be to the Father, and to the Son, and to the Holy Ghost: and glory to the Queen of heaven, with all the multitude of the heavenly hierarchy, for ever. Amen.

HYMN V

IN WHICH GOD IS PRAISED IN HIMSELF .

LET thy glorious and marvellous light bless thee for me, O my God; and the kingly splendour of thy most excellent Majesty praise thee.

Let the meet and seemly pomp of thy boundless glory bless thee: and the majestic energy of thine infinite power praise thee.

Let the princely splendour of thine eternal glory bless thee: and the glowing beauty of thy peerless honour praise thee.

Let the great deep of thy just judgment bless thee: and the unsearchable range of thine eternal wisdom praise thee.

Let the infinite number of thy manifold compassions bless thee: and the immeasurable height of thy tender mercies praise thee.

Let the bowels of thine infinite pity bless thee: and the overflowing abundance of thine unimaginable love praise thee.

Let the excessive love thou bearest to man bless thee: and the profuse bounty of thy most tender kindness praise thee.

Let the subduing force of thy exuberant sweetness bless thee: and the fulness of bliss which awaiteth thy chosen in thee praise thee.

Let the sublimity of thy dignity bless thee: and thy calm, everlasting unchangeableness praise thee.

Let the Godhead of thy most royal Trinity, the oneness of Essence and distinctness of Persons, bless thee for me: and thy sweet mutual indwelling and love, thy glorious and consummate felicity, praise thee.

Glory be to the Father, and to the Son, and to the Holy Ghost: and glory to the Queen of heaven, with all the multitude of the heavenly hierarchy, for ever. Amen.

OBLATION

ACCEPT, O Holy Trinity, the desires my lips have uttered and the glowing love of my heart has inspired, to set forth and praise thy magnificence. I offer them to thee in union with the ineffable praise which the three Persons of thy adorable Godhead offer one to another in manner and degree far above human comprehension. And so far as in me lies I cast my heart as a most worthless grain of incense into the golden censer of thy Divine Heart, wherein burns evermore to thy honour and glory the sweetest frankincense of eternal love; earnestly desiring and beseeching thee that, vile and unworthy as it is, it may be enkindled by the breath of thy spirit and consume away in thy worship and praise; and that the deep sighs I breathe towards thee from this valley of tears, because my hope is so long deferred, may be to thee an endless praise and glory. Amen.

HYMN OF PRAISE TO GOD

O HEIGHT inaccessible of wondrous power! O unfathomable depth of hidden wisdom! O boundless breadth of much-desired love! None but thyself can worthily praise thee, for thou alone knowest thine infinite magnificence, and thou knowest how thou oughtest to be praised. Wherefore, O Lord my God, may thine eternal Godhead, thy uncircumscribed Majesty, and thine infinite goodness, praise thee for me. O Lord my God, may thy loftiest wisdom, thy widest and most ample mercy, and thy most profound justice, praise thee for me. May thy greatness without limits, thy exquisite and penetrating sweetness, and thy most compassionate kindness, praise thee for me.

May all the names, all the titles, all the emblems, which can be said of thee or conceived of thee, bless thee, exult in thee, and magnify thee for me, and give thee thanks for all good things which thou hast ever bestowed, or shalt hereafter bestow, on me or on any one of thy creatures.

May the most adorable Humanity of Jesus Christ praise thee and exult in thee for me, O Lord my God. May his most holy life and conversation on earth, his most divine virtue and graces, his most precious Blood and tears, his cruel wounds and bruises, his most bitter passion and death, supply all the defects of my service, and worthily glorify thee.

May the most serene Queen of heaven, the most chaste Virgin Mary, magnify and extol thee, O God my Creator; and together with her the ten thousand times ten thousand companies of blessed spirits, and the countless host of thy saints: may they sing praises to thee for me for ever.

May our most holy Mother the Church sing to thee and exult in thee for me; may the seven most hallowed Sacraments praise thee;

may all the reverent ceremonies and rites of thy Church honour thee; may all her psalms and prayers praise thee, all her virtues and her holiness, all her sorrow and her love, all her longing and her desire wherewith she sighs unto thee in this valley of tears.

May all the gratuitous gifts of grace which thou hast ever conferred on me give thee thanks and praise; may all my powers of body and soul, my nerves and veins, my bones and my flesh, all my desire and all my groaning, my understanding, my memory and my will, my inmost heart with its wondrous beatings and throbs; may all unite to shout for joy to thee. I offer and resign to thee all these, beseeching thee that thou wouldest make me show forth thy praise and glory in time and in eternity. Amen.

THREE INCOMPARABLE ACTS OF PRAISE

Which our Lord taught to St. Mechtilde

I VENERATE and glorify thee, O most blessed Trinity, in union with that ineffable glory with which God the Father in his omnipotence honours the Son and the Holy Ghost for ever.

I magnify and bless thee, O most blessed Trinity, in union with that most reverent glory with which God the Son in his unsearchable wisdom glorifies the Father and the Holy Ghost for ever.

I adore and extol thee, O most blessed Trinity, in union with that most adequate and befitting glory with which the Holy Ghost in his unchangeable goodness extols the Father and the Son for ever. Amen.

AN EFFICACIOUS ACT OF PRAISE

every word of which has a special weight of meaning

O MOST compassionate Jesus, may all the virtue and efficacy of thy Divinity praise thee for me. May all the tender loving-kindness of thy Humanity satisfy to thee for me. May all the kingly splendour and majesty of the Trinity glorify, magnify, and honour thee in thyself for me, with that sublimest praise wherewith thou sufficest to thyself, and suppliest what is lacking to the praises of all thy creatures.

AN EFFICACIOUS METHOD OF LOVING AND PRAISING GOD

While St. Mechtilde was disquieted because she did not worthily honour and love God, our Lord said to her: When you desire to praise me, and cannot praise me as you would, say:

O GOOD Jesus, I praise thee: vouchsafe to supply for me whatsoever is lacking in my praise.

And if you wish to love me, say:

O GOOD Jesus, I love thee: vouchsafe to supply whatever is lacking in my love, and offer the love of thy Sacred Heart to God the Father for me.

And on another occasion he said to her: If you desire to praise me, repeat these few words:

GLORY be to thee, O most sweet, most noble, resplendent, peaceful, ineffable Trinity.

AN ACT OF CONGRATULATION MOST PLEASING TO
GOD

O MOST glorious God, I, the least of thy servants, congratulate thee, and rejoice with my whole heart that thou art and abidest unchangeably such and so great a God as thou art in thy Godhead and Essence, and shalt be evermore. I congratulate thee and rejoice with thee in thine infinite power and majesty. I rejoice and give thee thanks for thy great glory and thine inexpressible excellency. I rejoice and exult with my whole heart that all things are subject to thy sway, and that there is none that can resist thy will. And to express to thee my congratulations and my gratitude that thou art so great and so ineffable a God, I offer thee, in union with the sweetest Heart of Jesus and in my own name and that of all thy creatures, thy divine and infinite Essence with all the perfections, attributes, and qualities contained therein, in such manner and with such love as thou hast enabled us through thy love in the Holy Ghost. I desire and long that all creatures in heaven and in earth may acknowledge thee and love thee, and rejoice in thine infinite glory and blessedness; and I place them all before thee in spirit, and subject them to thee, and congratulate thee in their name. And since this falls far short of showing forth all thy praise, I beseech thee that thou wouldest vouchsafe to supply for thine own sake my lack of service, and that of all creatures, in loving thee and rejoicing in thee. And I offer to thee this splendour and fragrance of love and congratulation, together with all the glory, praise, and congratulation which the blessed spirits and souls of the just render thee with one consent, in thanksgiving for all the glory and the blessedness which thou dost enjoy for evermore. Amen.

SUBLIME ACT OF THANKSGIVING

From the devotions of St. Gertrude

BLESSED be thy goodness, O my God, and blessed be thy compassion, O thou one and true Godhead, thou one and holy Trinity, thou one and supreme God, for all the benefits and loving-kindnesses with which thy profuse and loving compassion has surrounded me, undeserving as I am. For all these I adore thee, I praise and bless thee, O my most tender Lord and God, in union with that supernal praise with which thou, O glorious Trinity, art thine own sufficient praise, which pours down from thee upon the blessed Humanity of our Lord Jesus Christ, upon his glorious Mother, and upon all holy angels and saints; and from them flows back again into its source in the abysses of thy Divinity. I give thee thanks for the love with which thou hast created and redeemed me, sanctified me, called me, preserved me, and endowed me with all manner of good things. And since praise is not seemly in the mouth of a sinner, I beseech thee, O sweetest Jesus, by that prevailing love wherewith thou sittest at the right hand of the Father, to pay for me to my God eternal, infinite, unfaltering, unceasing praises, such as thou alone canst pay, and such as thou knowest to be befitting his most dread glory and the honour of his Majesty, for all the good which has ever flowed forth upon me from the inexhaustible abyss of his Godhead. Break forth, therefore, O beloved Jesus, into such thanksgivings as thou alone canst utter; O my Lord, great and wonderful exceedingly, praise the Godhead in thyself, in me and for me, with all the might of thy Divinity and with all the love of thy Humanity, in the name and on behalf of all the universe thy hands have made.   Amen.

ACKNOWLEDGEMENT OF THE BENEFITS OF GOD

While saying this prayer, St. Gertrude received from the Son of God most gracious tokens of his love, and his promise that he would take her into his most intimate and special protection. Hence she learned that the Lord takes in a special manner under his protection all who gratefully recite this acknowledgement, and commit themselves to his divine Providence.

I GIVE thee thanks, O holy Father, with all my strength, through him who sitteth at thy right hand, for all the gifts I have ever received from thy munificent bounty; and I acknowledge that no power could have bestowed them on me but thine alone, who art all-powerful, and upholdest all creation.

I give thee thanks, most kind and gentle Jesus, and I confess, and will confess to my latest breath, that thou hast most wisely and well provided for me in body and in soul, in all things prosperous or adverse; and I acknowledge that no wisdom could thus embrace all my whole life but thy increated wisdom alone, O my most tender God, which reacheth from end to end mightily, and ordereth all things sweetly.

I give thee thanks, O good and quickening Spirit, the Comforter, through him who was by thy cooperation made flesh in the Virgin's womb, that thou dost in all things so sweetly anticipate me, unworthy as I am, with the blessings of thy gratuitous bounty; and I acknowledge that no goodness could thus diffuse itself but thy ineffable goodness, in which all good things are contained, from which they proceed, and together with which they are received. And as thou hast hitherto and always provided for me, so I confidently hope and rely that thou wilt provide for me to the end through thy divine goodness, to which I most devoutly commend myself. Amen.

PROFESSION OF FAITH

O MY God, thou ancient and absolute truth, I (N.) believe with my heart, confess with my mouth, and profess by my actions, that I most firmly believe all and every article of faith which the holy Roman Church proposes to us to be believed, and that I will believe them to the end of my life. And although I can in no wise understand how the truths which the faith delivers to us are possible. nevertheless I bring my understanding into the captivity of the obedience of Christ, I revere these most sacred mysteries with profound submission, and I beseech thee to render them availing to my salvation. And even as I now profess this faith, so I vow, promise, and swear, in presence of all the holy angels and saints, and above all in thy presence, O most holy Trinity, that I desire to live and die in the same. So help me God and these his holy Gospels. "In the beginning was the Word, and the Word was with God, and the Word was God."

Here commend thy faith to God, as follows: for our Lord revealed to St. Mechtilde that those who do so shall be preserved from temptations against the faith to their lives' end.

I COMMEND this my faith to thine omnipotence, O eternal Father, beseeching thee that thou wouldst so strengthen me therein with thy divine strength, that I may never depart from it nor waver in it.

I commend it to thine unsearchable wisdom, O only-begotten Son, beseeching thee that thou wouldst so enlighten me with the light of thy knowledge, that I may never be led astray by the spirit of error.

I commend it likewise to thy most compassionate goodness, O Holy Ghost the Comforter, beseeching thee that this my faith may so work in me by charity, that at the hour of my death it may be found perfect and entire.

TRUST IN GOD

Our Lord said to St. Mechtilde: Of a truth it greatly pleases me that men should confidently expect great things from me, for it is impossible that a man should fail to obtain that which he believes and hopes for. Therefore it is good for a man to hope great things from me, and to confide sincerely in me. ¶ *Our Lord gave also a like assurance to St. Gertrude.*

O GOD of my heart, my only hope and refuge, I, the poorest of thy creatures and infinitely unworthy of the least good at thy hands, do yet so confidently hope in thy tender kindness, that I have no manner of doubt that as thou knowest how to succour and aid me, so thou both canst and wilt be with me in all things. I know, indeed, O compassionate God, that if thou wert to deal with me as I have deserved, I could expect no grace at thy hand, but only manifold rebuke and punishment; but since I know that thy goodness is so exuberant that thou art wont to do good even to thy worst enemies, I most firmly believe and trust that thou wilt not forsake me in my distresses and miseries, but wilt provide for me with a care and generosity which I should vainly look for in my dearest friend.

O most loving God, although my sins are so manifold and so grievous that they deserve a thousand hells, yet by reason of thine infinite goodness I so securely expect from thee remission of them all, provided only they grieve me, as in deed and in truth they do, that I could more easily doubt my own existence than the certainty of this remission. O infinite goodness, so tender is my confidence in thee, that even if I had sinned a thousand times more than I have, and knew that thine anger was fiercely kindled against me, yet, could I

choose my own judge, I would choose none
other than thee. In thee alone, and in none
other than thee, would I trust, and I should
more certainly hope for mercy at thy hand
than from my best and dearest friend. For if
I had sinned as often and as grievously against
any one of my friends as I have against thee,
I am most sure that I could not hope for
pardon, even from the most tender and compassionate of mothers. Yea, had I been so
rebellious and so unloving to my own mother
as I have been to thee, she would have cast
me off for ever. But thou, notwithstanding all
the many and grievous insults I have heaped
upon thee, and notwithstanding all my many
and grievous negligences in thy service, dost
still cherish and sustain me.

And dost thou think, O most loving Father,
that I have the smallest doubt that I shall attain to everlasting bliss? Do thou thyself for-
bid. For my hope of attaining that bliss rests
not on my own merits, but on the faithful
promise of thy Only-begotten, and on his most
abundant and exuberant merits, which he has
communicated and made over unto his elect.
And hence I abound with so great joy and
consolation, because I seem already to possess
that for which I so eagerly long. For thy Son,
who has promised me salvation and his merits,
which are its title and its price, is most faithful,
nor can any word which has gone forth from
his mouth be revoked or fail. Vouchsafe, O

eternal Father, to increase in me this hope and trust which I give into thy merciful keeping, until I see thee in thy unfading eternity, and hope be lost in fruition. Amen.

LOVE OF GOD

It was revealed to St. Gertrude that when a soul which loves God turns to him with ardent affection and desire, if it were possible, to make reparation to him for all the insults and affronts whereby his honour is outraged, and expresses to him all its yearning tenderness, his anger is appeased, and he spares the world of sinners. For one loving soul obtains more from God for all the faithful living and departed than ten thousand who are cold and unloving.

O MY God, most worthy object of my love, my supreme and infinite Good, I love thee and will love thee for ever and ever; I embrace thee with all the affections of my heart, with the strong embrace of love, for thou art my sweetest and much-desired Good, thou my perennial peace and sweetness, thou the sufficing portion of my soul. O thou most gentle, most ravishing, most beloved Lord, thou art the life of my soul, thou the jubilee of my heart, my God, my Love, the chosen One of all my vows. I love thee, O my sweetness, my joy, my delight; I love thee with all my soul and with all my strength, but, alas, not as I ought, not as I would. Would that I could love thee a thousand-fold more; would that I could love thee with an infinite love! Pierce my heart, O sweetest God, with the arrow of thy love, and wound it with the languishing wound of thy direction. Grant that I may love thee, O my Lord; for without thee I cannot love thee. Oh, could I gather all created hearts, and contain them all in my heart, with all their affections and their love, how would I love thee then, O my fairest Love! Oh, wouldst thou give me but for one hour the glowing love of Seraphim, that I might be inflamed with the ardour of that impetuous love and enkindle it in every heart of men! And how great is my grief that thou, my tender Love, art not loved! Alas, how I mourn that thou, my sweet Love, art neglected and despised, and above all that thou art so cruelly offended and outraged! I condole with thee, O my God and my Love, on all the injuries and insults which are heaped on thee; and, were I able, I would most gladly make reparation to thee for all the outrages and wrongs done to thine honour; yea, for thy love I would gladly suffer to my dying hour all the pangs of holy desire which the heart of man hath suffered or shall suffer to the end of the world, if so I might offer thee a more worthy shelter within my soul, and make amends to thee for all the contempt and ignominy which thy peerless and excelling dignity sustains at the hands of ungrateful men. Amen.

ASPIRATIONS OF A LOVING SOUL

He who ardently desires and firmly resolves to love and praise me more than I am praised and loved by any other creature shall undoubtedly, said our Lord to St. Gertrude, receive an abundant reward from my divine bounty; a reward often times greater than that which he could obtain by good works.

O GOD of my heart, I love thee with all my heart, and I would that I could love thee a thousand-fold more. Would that I could praise and love thee beyond every other of thy creatures; that I could give thee thanks and condole with thee, and practise all virtues in greatest perfection: most eagerly and most gladly would I do so, according to the sovereign good pleasure of thy divine Heart.

O my sweet Love, could I bring before thee, my Lord and my God, all men in whom thou hast vouchsafed to take thy delights, I would most gladly go barefoot throughout the world, and bring to thee in my arms all in whose hearts thou dost deign and delight to dwell, that I might thus satisfy the yearnings of thy infinite, thy divine love. And moreover, were it possible, I would divide my heart into as many fragments as there are men on the earth, that I might communicate to them all a holy resolve to serve and obey thee to the joy and content of thy divine Heart.

O God, worthy of an infinite love, I have nothing which can be commensurate with thy dignity; but such is my desire towards thee, that if I had all that thou hast, I would gladly and thankfully resign all to thee.

HOLOCAUST

When St. Gertrude had once offered this holocaust to God, our Lord Jesus Christ appeared to her, bearing her oblation and setting it forth before the Blessed Trinity as a gift of exceeding price; and as he passed through the midst of heaven the whole heavenly host knelt before him in reverence for that choice oblation. Whence she understood that whenever any one offers his prayers or his desires to God, the whole company of heaven bears them up to the throne of God as gifts most precious and acceptable; and that whenever the merits of Jesus Christ are added thereunto, the saints bow and adore them as aforesaid.

O GOD of glorious majesty, Ruler of heaven and earth, I thy most unworthy creature offer thee, upon the most sacred altar of the sweetest Heart of Jesus Christ, myself with all that I am, all I have, all I can do, together with every good gift which thou hast ever bestowed on me from thine unfathomable, overflowing bounty. Moreover I offer thee all the treasures and the wealth of this world, all kingdoms, royalties, princedoms, honours, and dignities, with this intention: that were they all mine, I would distribute them to thy poor, or employ them in other pious uses, that for very love of thee I might abide with joy in my present state of poverty.

Further, I offer to thee on the same altar all the virtues, devotions, merits, and holiness of all the just; all the affliction, the crosses, the poverty, and want of all the poor, the afflicted, and the sick; all the pangs, the torments, the wounds, the bloodshedding, and the death of all martyrs; all the penance, the mortification, the fastings, vigils, and austerities of all confessors; all the love, the continence, the purity of all virgins: and I offer them all to thee with this intention: that were they all mine, I would do and suffer them all with most pure intention for thy glory.

Thirdly, I offer thee all the whole fulness of grace and glory, transcending all human thought, wherewith thou hast so super-abundantly enriched thy saints in heaven, and especially the most glorious Virgin Mary, Mother of thy only-begotten Son. And above all these I offer thee the virtues and merits which thy Son manifested on earth, and all the gifts of grace, drawn from the infinitely exuberant treasury of the most Holy Trinity, which thou hast bestowed on his most sacred Humanity. For all which I desire, on behalf of all in heaven and earth, and through the most sacred and blessed Heart of thy Son, which gives forth its ravishing harmony at the touch of the Holy

Ghost the Comforter, to sing unto thee praises and thanksgivings, and thus to give thee back thine own.

Lastly, I offer thee the priceless ineffable abundance of riches and perfections which thy divine Essence contains within itself, and which one divine Person communicates to another in sweetest, most transcending, and unimaginable manner. For all which I give thee thanks with all my heart and strength; I congratulate thee that thou dost contain within thyself and for thyself such inexhaustible treasures and delights, and dost perpetually and for ever communicate them to thine elect. Wherefore, O my King, live for ever, and enjoy evermore that bliss which is thyself, and vouchsafe to bestow on us wretched exiles in this valley of tears some crumbs from thy heavenly table. Amen.

ACT OF RESIGNATION

It was revealed to St. Gertrude that those who submit and conform themselves entirely to the divine will, desiring above all things that the adorable will of God may be most fully done in all that concerns them whether in body or in soul, touch the Sacred Heart most sensibly. For such perfect resignation is an acknowledgement of God's sovereignty, and gives him as much honour as is given to an earthly king when the crown of his realm is set on his head.

O MOST holy Father, I thy poor and vile creature entirely renounce my own will, and offer and resign myself to thy most holy will and pleasure; above all delights of this world, I wish and desire that thy most adorable, most placid will may be perfectly done in my, by me, in all that concerns me whether in body or in soul, in time and in eternity. And to this end I would readily submit all the members of my body to suffering of any kind and degree.

O my God, wert thou to give me fullest choice of asking all I wish, and didst thou swear to me by thyself that thou wouldst grant my petition in all things, I would neither desire nor ask aught else than that thy most adorable will may be perfectly done in me and in every creature of thine, according to thy supreme and faultless good pleasure. Wherefore, in union with that resignation with which Jesus committed himself wholly to thy will in the garden of Olives, and in union with his affection and his intention, I say from his heart and in his words: Not my will, but thine be done, O most holy Father, in time and in eternity. Amen.

Should any affliction threaten you, add the following words, which are most pleasing to God, as he condescended to reveal to St. Gertrude. If any one, says she, offers his whole will to the will of God when he knows that affliction is coming on him, his offering will be as ac-

ceptable to God as though, during the Passion of Jesus, he had allayed the anguish of his wounds with fragrant ointments.

A ND more especially, O good Jesus, I offer and resign myself to thee, in perfect readiness of will to bear that affliction which I foresee coming upon me; I will accept it with unshaken will as from thy Hand, and I will bear it with what patience I can; in union with that love wherewith thou didst accept all thine afflictions from thy Father's Hand, and didst offer them to him again in ineffable gratitude; beseeching thee that thou wouldest grant me fortitude and patience, that I may manfully endure, to thy eternal glory and to the welfare and peace of all the world.—Amen.

PART IV

PRAYERS TO JESUS CHRIST

WREATH OF GEMS

Composed of three beads of gold and fifteen of silver. While St. Gertrude was offering this wreath of salutations in honour of the name of Jesus, she seemed to see them under the form of roses hung around with golden bells, the fragrance and tuneful harmony of which touched the Sacred Heart with ineffable delight. Those which had been recited with devout intention gave forth a most ravishing melody, while those which had been said carelessly uttered a low and wailing sound. And the Lord said to her: Whenever any one prays to me, Hail, sweetest Jesus, &c., *the depth of the sweetness of my Godhead is stirred within me, and there spreads itself before me an odour of wondrous fragrance, which I shed down on him who repeats these words.*

FIRST GOLDEN BEAD

HAIL, most loving Jesus, life-giving Germ of the divine Honour, unfading flower of human dignity, my consummate and my only salvation. Thou art my Creator and my Redeemer, and thou hast so loved me as to leave all thy bliss and thy glory, and to purchase me for thyself with the anguish of thy death.

Five silver beads

1. Hail, sweetest Jesus, most precious pearl of the most holy Trinity, with whose price the world has been redeemed.

2. Hail, most tender Jesus, refulgent splendour of the Father's glory, who with the light of thy countenance dost enlighten and quicken thine elect in the heavenly country.

3. Hail, most amiable Jesus, flashing effulgence from the sun of Justice, who dost inflame the hearts of angels and saints with the fire of thy love.

4. Hail, most noble Jesus, living Image of thy Father's substance, who dost make all those who cleave to thee partakers of thy divine nature.

5. Hail, most renowned Jesus, Morning Star of thy Church, who enlightenest the darkness of the world, and scatterest all the thick darkness of sin.

SECOND GOLDEN BEAD

HAIL, Jesus, Bridegroom most beauteous in the charm of thy Divinity, I salute thee and embrace thee with the affection of all thy creatures, and kiss thee with my mouth, thou Wound of love.

Five silver beads

1. Hail, Jesus, fairer than the sons of men, Orient pearl born in the ocean of the God-

head of the Father, whose generation no created intelligence can declare.

2. Hail, Jesus, sweeter than honey and the honeycomb, heavenly manna of wondrous sweetness, who dost refresh and satisfy every hungry soul.

3. Hail, Jesus most resplendent, glowing Fire of uncreated love, who dost lighten and bear the burden of human toil and misery.

4. Hail, Jesus most gentle, sweet channel of heavenly streams, who dost take away the bitterness of every soul in anguish.

5. Hail, priceless Jesus, treasure-house of the divine Essence, who dost enrich the poverty of our nature. Amen.

THIRD GOLDEN BEAD

HAIL, Jesus, full of grace, mercy is with thee, and thou art blessed among the sons of men; and blessed be thy most Holy Name, thy Life and thy Passion. O sweet Jesus, Son of God, have mercy on us sinners now and in the hour of our death. Amen.

Five silver beads

1. Hail, Jesus, Spouse and Crown of Virgins, we praise thee for ever, whose love made thee Son of the Virgin.

2. Hail, Jesus, Ruler of all things, fairer in thy beauty than the sons of men, we acknowledge and worship thee as our most clement Lord.

3. Hail, Jesus, wondrous splendour of the Godhead, wonder of wonders, who dost blot out all the sins of the world.

4. Hail, Jesus, our consolation, who dost lay open to us the treasury of the riches of God, thou true refuge of the poor, and comfort of the afflicted.

5. Hail, Jesus, glory of angels, living Fountain, light of all minds, who dost transcend all joy and all desire. Amen.

OBLATION

O GOOD Jesus, my love, my joy, and my sweetness, my soul loves thee alone; for thee alone doth my longing spirit pine. For thou art more glorious than the sun, fairer than the moon, more radiant than the dawn, more brilliant than the stars. Thou art whiter than the lily, more ruddy than the rose, more vigorous than the hyacinth, and more fragrant than earth's most fragrant flowers. Thou art sweeter than all sweetness, more tender than all affection, more exquisite than all dainties, beloved above all love. Thou alone art great and to be praised, thou alone art sweet and to be loved, thou alone art fair and pleasant, thou alone beauteous and full of delight, thou alone hast no counterpart or equal in heaven or in earth. Wherefore, in token of my love, I offer thee this wreath of gems, and present it to thee on the golden altar of thy divine Heart, in union with that unceasing melody of praise wherewith the whole company of heaven worships thee. And since this my meagre, barren praise is altogether unworthy of thee, O true Love of my heart, do thou thyself perform the stately solemnity of thy praise; and together with thee let all the ranks of heaven rejoice and sing aloud for that greatest, sweetest blessing, that thou art my God, and that thou dost condescend to be acknowledged, and loved, and praised by me, the refuse and offscouring of thy creatures. Amen.

LOVING AFFECTIONS TOWARDS JESUS

This prayer was revealed to St. Gertrude during an unusually abundant influx of grace and light. Our Lord said to her: Whoever repeats this prayer shall receive the grace to know me more intimately, and shall receive into his soul the splendour of my Divinity, even as he who holds up to the sun a mirror of pure gold collects therein the dazzling effulgence of its rays.

O THOU most excelling King of kings, Prince of glory, my loving Jesus, thou art the life of my soul; may all the affection of my heart be inflamed with the ardour of thy love, and for ever united to thee. May it sink back baffled and exhausted when it would love aught but what tends to thee alone; for thou art the brilliance of all colour, the savour of all dainties, the fragrance of all odours, the charm of all melody, the soothing repose of all love. O thou overflowing abyss of Divinity, in thee is pleasure most enrapturing, from thee ever-gushing streams of plenty spread around, towards thee a gentle force irresistibly attracts, through thee our souls are inundated with thrilling gladness. O King of kings most worthy, sovereign Lord of all, Prince most glorious, most clement Ruler, thou most mighty Protector; thou art the vivifying germ of human dignity, O most wonderful in thy working, gentlest of Teachers, Wisest in counsel, most kind and effectual Helper, Friend faithful unto death. No union is so intimate, so beatific, as thine, O thou transporting, soothing Lover of souls, most tender and chaste Spouse of thy chosen. Thou art the spring Flower of noble gracefulness, O my brother most fair, ruddy, and comely in thy youth, most winning companion, Host most munificent in thy provision; I choose thee in preference to all creatures, for thy sake I renounce all pleasure, for thee I run with joy to meet all adversity, and in all I do I seek no other praise than thine. I acknowledge with heart and mouth that thou art the root from which these and all good things spring. With the energy of thy fervour I unite my intention to that of thy most availing prayer, that in virtue of this divine union every movement of rebellion may be quelled and crushed within me, and that I may be led by thee to the summit and pinnacle of perfection. Amen.

PRAYER TO THE NAME OF JESUS

O GOOD Jesus, O most compassionate Jesus, O Jesus Son of God and of the Virgin Mary, full of mercy and of pity; O sweet Jesus, have mercy on me according to thy great mercy. O most clement Jesus, I implore thee, by that thy precious Blood which thou hast shed for sinners, that thou wouldst wash away all my iniquities, and look down upon me, wretched and unworthy, humbly seeking thy forgiveness and invoking this holy Name of Jesus. O Name of Jesus, name of sweetness! Name of Jesus, name most full of delight! Name of Jesus, name most lovely! For what is Jesus but Saviour? Wherefore, O Jesus, for thy holy Name's sake, be to me Jesus, and save me. Suffer me not to be lost, whom thou hast redeemed with thy Precious Blood. O good Jesus, let not mine iniquity destroy me, the work of thy almighty goodness. O Jesus most benignant, have mercy on me in this day of mercy, that thou condemn me not in the day of judgment. O most compassionate Jesus, if thy stern justice incline to condemn me, I make my appeal and my refuge in thy most pitiful mercy. O most loving Jesus, Jesus most ardently longed for, Jesus most gentle and meek, O Jesus, Jesus, Jesus, receive me into the number of thy chosen. O Jesus, the salva-

tion of those who believe in thee; O Jesus, the
trust of those who flee for refuge unto thee;
O Jesus, the sweetness of those who love thee;
grant that I may love thee, and cleave faithfully to thee, and after this most miserable
life come to thee in peace. Amen.

PETITION TO JESUS

*That by his most holy life and conversation he
would make satisfaction for our transgressions.*

O TENDER Jesus, full of pity and of mercy,
who never despisest the sighing of the
wretched, to thee I betake myself, imploring
thy clemency. Speak thou for me, supply thou
for me; for I confess unto thee all my sins.
By the sinless tears of thy most glorious eyes,
wash away all the stains of my sinful eyes.
By the gentle pity of thy blessed ears, wash
away all the iniquities of my sinful ears. By
the thrilling energy of the sweet words of thy
blessed lips, wash away all the offences of my
polluted lips. By the perfection of thine actions
and by the wounds in thy hands, wash away
all the offences of my impious hands. By the
aching weariness of thy blessed feet, and by
the cruel holes of the nails, wash away all the
defilement of my sinful feet. By the pure intention of thy most holy thoughts, and by the
glowing love of thy pierced Heart, wash away
all the guiltiness of my evil thoughts and of
my wicked heart. By the matchless innocence

of thy life, and by thy unspotted holiness, destroy all the foulness of my corrupt life. By the priceless fountain of thy most Precious Blood, wash away, cleanse and efface every defilement of my heart and soul, that by thy most holy merits I may be found clean from sin, and be henceforward enabled to keep all thy commandments perfectly and spotlessly. Amen.

FIVE SUBLIME ASPIRATIONS TO JESUS CHRIST

which he himself taught to St. Mechtilde.

O SWEET Jesus, I sigh unto thee in union with that glory which floweth down from thee upon all thy saints, to make up what is lacking in the glory which all creatures ought to give thee.

O compassionate Jesus, I sigh unto thee in union with the gratitude which riseth towards thee from the hearts of thy saints, when they give thanks to thee for the gifts thou hast bestowed on them.

O meek Jesus, I sigh unto thee by reason of my sins and those of all men, in union with that patience with which thou dost support and endure the iniquities of us all.

O amiable Jesus, I sigh unto thee in union with that divine yearning which thou hadst on earth for the salvation of men, earnestly craving every good gift needful to men for thy glory and for their salvation.

O good Jesus, I sigh unto thee in union with all the prayer which has ever gone forth from thy divine Heart, and from the hearts of all saints, for all the faithful, living and departed. Amen.

OBLATION OF THE MERITS OF CHRIST FOR OUR SINS

When our Lord, at the request of St. Gertrude, had presented this oblation to God the Father, she appeared clothed in garments of white and red, with ornaments of wonderful richness. And, indeed, this prayer is of singular efficacy, and should be frequently repeated.

O MOST compassionate Jesus, since by reason of thine unsearchable wisdom thou knowest the extent of human frailty more clearly and fully than I or any one can know it, I implore thee to have manifold compassion on my manifold frailty, and to vouchsafe to supply all my defects and shortcomings. Offer to thy most gracious Father, O pitiful Jesus, the most becoming silence of thy holy lips, in expiation of all the sin I have committed, and in supply of all the good I have omitted, by vain and frivolous conversation. Offer, O good Jesus, the modesty of thy most holy ears, for all the sins I have committed by hearing. Offer also the reserve of thy eyes, for all the stains which I have contracted by wandering and forbidden looks. Offer the caution and deliberation of thy Hands and thy Feet, for all the sins which I have committed in my daily actions or in my daily walk. Lastly, O most loving Jesus, offer to his glorious Majesty thy deified Heart, for all the sins which I have committed by thought, will, or desire. Amen.

PRAISE OF JESUS IN THE ALLELVIA

St. Gertrude said to our Lord on Easter Day: Teach me, O thou gentlest Teacher, how I may most devoutly praise thee in the Alleluia. She received this answer: You may well and suitably praise me by uniting your intention in the following manner to that of the heavenly host, who unceasingly sing Alleluia to my glory.

I PRAISE thee, O my Jesus, in union with that all-transcending praise wherewith all thy saints extol, in rapturous harmony, the thrilling influx of the Divinity into thy deific Humanity, now that it is transfigured in unfading glory, in reward of the manifold bitterness of the Passion and Death thou didst endure for man's salvation.

I praise thee, O my Jesus, in union with that all-transcending praise, wherewith all thy saints extol the ravishing delight of that glad everlasting spring, wherein the eyes of thy Humanity feast in the green pastures of the one, whole, supreme, and undivided Trinity.

I praise thee, O my Jesus, in union with that all-transcending praise, wherewith all thy saints extol that most tranquil delight with which the ears of thy deified Humanity are soothed, in the ineffable endearments of the ever-adorable Trinity and the unwearying praises of angels and saints.

I praise thee, O my Jesus, in union with that all-transcending praise, wherewith all thy saints extol the entrancing fragrance which exhales from the Bosom of the most Holy Trinity, for the refreshment and delight of thy sacred and immortal Humanity.

I praise thee, O my Jesus, in union with that all-transcending praise, wherewith all thy saints extol with one accord the magnificent, the incomprehensible, inestimably precious influx of the Divinity into thy deific Humanity, which, now immortal and impassible, receives, in lieu of those mortal and passible sensations which it lacks, a double delight and joy from the divine influx.

A TENDER SALUTATION OF JESUS

This brief salutation was very familiar to St. Gertrude, because it made reparation to our Lord for the outrages he receives from men. Wherefore you will do well to follow her example, and repeat it frequently before the Crucifix.

HAIL, thou quickening germ of divine honour. Hail, unwithering flower of human dignity, thou most loving Jesus. I salute and embrace thee with all the joy and delight of thy Divinity, and with the affections of all mankind; and I commend myself to the sweetest Wound of thy sacred Heart. Amen.

SALUTATION OF THE WOUNDS OF JESUS

When St. Gertrude had recited this prayer 5466 times in honour of all the Wounds of our Lord Jesus, he appeared to her in vision, having on each Wound a rose flashing with a golden splendour, and greeted her tenderly, saying: Behold, I will appear to thee in this refulgent form at the hour of thy death, and I will cover all thy sins, and adorn thee with a glory like that with which thou hast adorned my Wounds by thy salutations; and all who use this or any similar devotion shall receive the like favour. In order to make up this number, and become a partaker of this promise of Christ, you may say the following prayer five times a day for three years, adding the oblation which our Lord directed St. Mechtilde to repeat after each division of five.

GLORY be to thee, most gracious, sweetest, most benign, sovereign, transcending, effulgent, and ever-peaceful Trinity, for the roseate Wounds of Jesus Christ, my chosen and only Love.

OBLATION

To be said after each five repetitions

O LORD Jesus Christ, Son of the living God, accept this prayer with that surpassing love with which thou didst endure all the Wounds of thy most holy Body. And have mercy on me, and on all sinners, and on all the faithful, living and departed. Grant unto them grace and mercy, remission of sins, and everlasting life. Amen.

ANOTHER SALUTATION OF THE WOUNDS OF JESUS

which the Holy Ghost taught to St. Mechtilde, and which she had neither heard nor known before.

HAIL, most precious Wounds of Jesus, in the omnipotence of the Father, who decreed you; hail, in the wisdom of the Son, who endured you; hail, in the goodness of the Holy Ghost, who through you accomplished the work of human redemption. To you I commend myself, in you I hide myself, into you I plunge myself, that in your shelter I may be secure from the destroyer. Amen.

SALUTATION OF THE HEART OF JESUS

while St. Mechtilde was meditating in the bitterness of her heart how negligently she had

served God, our Lord said to her: To compen-
sate and make good all thy former negligences,
salute my Heart in the divine Goodness, as
follows:

H AIL., sweetest Heart of Jesus, most tuneful
instrument of the Holy Trinity. Hail,
Heart of Jesus, flowing with honey, living
stream of all goodness and all grace. Hail,
loving Heart of Jesus, most noble treasury of
the riches of God. I bless and salute thee a
thousand and a thousand-fold in the divine
Goodness, that thou art the Fountain and
Source whence all good and all mercy stream
forth. O noble and precious Heart of Jesus
Christ, I salute and adore thee, through the
mutual complacency of the worshipful Trinity,
in the abundance of all graces, wherewith thou
dost evermore inundate all holy and devout
souls, whom thou hast so often bedewed and
inebriated with the torrent of thy divine
pleasures.

O Heart of Jesus, Heart most sweet; Heart
of Jesus, Heart most precious; Heart of Jesus,
Heart most worthy of love; O Heart flowing
with sweetness, abounding with pity, overflowing with charity; in thy most hidden recesses I plunge my spirit, and in the great
deep of thy mercy I bury all the burden of my
iniquity and my negligence. To thee I offer all
my labours and my toils, to thee I dedicate all
my anguish and my misery, to thee I commend my life, and the end of my life. O Heart,

sweet-smelling spikenard, frankincense most fragrant, most worthy and adequate sacrifice; offer thyself upon the golden altar of pro- pitiation, to compensate for all the days of my life wherein I have brought no fruit to God.

I bless thee, O most kingly Heart of Jesus, in that love wherewith the Holy Ghost formed thee of the most chaste blood of the Virgin Mary. I glorify thee, O sweetest Heart of Jesus, in that love wherewith the Holy Trinity adorned thee with all heavenly gifts. I magnify thee, O gentlest Heart of Jesus, in that love wherewith thou didst glow for all the human race. I adore thee, O most benign Heart of Jesus, in that love whereby thou wast broken upon the cross. I extol thee, O Heart of Jesus, most true and faithful, in that love wherewith thou didst will to be thrust through with the lance and to shed forth Blood and Water.

Wherefore, O transcendently glorious Trin- ity, I praise thee, I glorify and bless thee, through that surpassingly blessed Heart, that thou hast willed and desired to bestow on it such manifold gifts and such an abundance of grace: and with all possible love and rever- ence I offer to thy divine Majesty that Heart, so ravishing in sweetness, and so supremely and alone worthy, through the fulness of divine complacency and the ineffable perfection of manifold bliss, with which thou hast filled it for ever; and I beseech thee, that thou wouldst vouchsafe for his sake to pardon whatever I have done that is wrong, and to supply and perfect whatever I have omitted or done negligently. Amen.

LITANY OF THE MOST HOLY NAME OF JESUS

LORD have mercy.
Christ have mercy.
Lord have mercy.
Jesus hear us.
Jesus graciously hear us.
O God the Father, of heaven,
O God the Son, Redeemer of the world,
O God the Holy Ghost,
Holy Trinity, One God,
Jesus, Son of the living God,
Jesus, Son of the Virgin Mary,
Jesus, Son of David,
Jesus, most kind,
Jesus, most loving,
Jesus, most meek,
Jesus, most gentle,
Jesus, most mild,
Jesus, most sweet,
Jesus, full of pity,
Jesus, most amicable,
Jesus, most merciful,
Jesus, most bountiful,
Jesus, most gracious,
Jesus, most lovely,
Jesus, most noble,
Jesus, most renowned,

Have mercy on us.

Jesus, most glorious,

Jesus, chosen of ten thousand,

Jesus, Splendour of the Father's glory,

Jesus, Figure of the Father's substance,

Jesus, Spouse of chaste souls, flowing with delights,

Jesus, vivifying Germ of Divine Honour,

Jesus, unfading Flower of human dignity,

By thy sweetest Name,

By the compassion of thy Divine Heart,

By the union of the Divinity with thy Humanity,

By the love wherewith thou didst come down from heaven and complete the work of human redemption,

By the love wherewith thou didst will to be laid in the manger,

By the love wherewith thou didst suck the chaste breasts of the Virgin Mary,

By the love wherewith for thirty-three years thou didst endure all our miseries,

By the love wherewith thou didst undergo a most bitter death,

By the love wherewith thou didst will thy Heart to be pierced,

By the love wherewith at thy resurrection thou didst glorify thy sacred Body,

By the love wherewith thou hast placed thy Humanity at the right hand of the Father,

By the love wherewith thou dost make glad thy Saints with the comeliness of thy Face,

Have mercy on us.

By the love wherewith thou dost show thy
  deified Heart to the Father for us sin-
  ners,
By the mutual love of thy Divinity and thy
  Humanity,
Jesus Christ,
Lamb of God. who takest away the sins of
  the world, *Spare us, O Jesus.*
Lamb of God, who takest away the sins of
  the world, *Graciously hear us, O Jesus.*
Lamb of God, who takest away the sins of
  the world, *Have mercy on us, O Jesus.*
V. Graciously hear us, O Jesus, Saviour of
  the world.
R. To whom nothing is impossible, save to
  refuse mercy to the wretched.

Have mercy on us.

Let us pray

O MOST tender Jesus, true Sweetness of all
  who flee to thee for refuge, receive this
my prayer which I devoutly offer thee through
thy sweetest Heart, to the everlasting praise of
thy sweetest Name; beseeching thee, by that
love wherewith thou didst will to receive that
most holy Name and to make it so sweet and
so lovely to all the faithful, that by the virtue
of that most sacred Name Jesus thou wouldst
vouchsafe to strengthen me in all temptations,
and to be with me in my last hour, according
to thy faithful promise: who livest and reignest, &c.

PART V

ON THE PASSION OF OUR LORD

TEN PRAYERS OF DEVOUT AFFECTIONS

in which our Lord's Passion is pleaded with him.

It was revealed to St. Gertrude that reading and meditations on the Passion are far more useful and efficacious than all other spiritual exercises. As those who handle flour cannot avoid contracting some whiteness, so no one, however imperfect his devotion may be, can occupy his mind with the Passion of our Lord without receiving some benefit therefrom. And, however cold and lukewarm our devotion, our Lord will look upon us with greater long-suffering and mercy if we never omit the memory of his Passion.

FIRST PRAYER

O LORD Jesus Christ, the eternal Sweetness and Jubilee of those who love thee, remember all the presentiment of grief thou didst endure from the moment of thy conception, and especially at thy entrance into thy Passion, when thou didst say: *My soul is sorrowful, even unto death;* and when, by reason of overwhelming dread and anguish and grief, thou didst sweat as it were drops of blood trickling down upon the ground. Remember all the bitterness of thy sorrow when thou wast seized upon by the Jews, accused by false witnesses, condemned by thy three judges, buffeted and smitten, spit upon, scourged, and crowned with thorns. O sweetest Jesus, I implore thee, by all the sorrows and insults thou didst endure, have mercy on me a sinner. Amen.

SECOND PRAYER

O JESUS, Paradise of the delights of God, remember now all the dread and sorrow thou didst endure when Pilate pronounced on thee sentence of death; when the godless soldiers laid the heavy cross on thy shoulders, and fastened thee thereon with rude and blunted nails, cruelly stretching thy sacred limbs so that all thy bones could be numbered: I beseech thee, vouchsafe to pronounce a merciful sentence on me in the day of judgment, and deliver me from all punishment. Amen.

THIRD PRAYER

O JESUS, heavenly Physician, remember now the languor and the pain thou didst endure when lifted upon the cross, when all thy bones were out of joint, so that no sorrow was like to thy sorrow, because, from the sole of thy foot to the top of thy head, there was no soundness in thee. And notwithstanding thou didst put away the feeling of all thine own griefs, and pray to thy Father for thine enemies, saying: *Father, forgive them; for they know not what they do.* By this thy charity and thy mercy, grant that the dignity and worth of thy Passion may be the entire remission of all my sins. Amen.

FOURTH PRAYER

O JESUS, Mirror of the eternal splendour, remember now that sadness which filled thy heart when thou didst behold in the mirror of thy Divinity the reprobation of the wicked and the multitude of the lost; and by the depth of the compassion thou didst then feel for lost and despairing sinners, and by the mercy thou didst show to the robber on the cross, saying: *This day thou shalt be with me in Paradise,* I beseech thee, O compassionate Jesus, show me thy mercy in the hour of my death. Amen.

FIFTH PRAYER

O JESUS, King most beloved, remember now all the mournful desolation of thy heart, when thou, the tenderest and most faithful of friends, wast forsaken by all, and mocked as thou hungest on the cross; when thou didst find none to comfort thee but thy beloved Mother, who stood by thy cross to the last, and whom thou didst commend to thy disciple, saying: *Woman, behold thy son,* and to thy disciple: *Behold thy Mother.* I beseech thee, O compassionate Jesus, by that sword of anguish which then pierced her heart, do thou condole with me and console me in all my tribulations. Amen.

SIXTH PRAYER

O JESUS, inexhaustible Fountain of pity, remember now that bitterness which thou didst endure when, all thy strength being exhausted and thy Sacred Body dried up, thou didst feel that burning thirst, and hadst not one drop of water to cool thy parched tongue, but only vinegar upon hyssop; I beseech thee that thou wouldest extinguish in me the thirst of carnal concupiscence and worldly delights. Amen.

SEVENTH PRAYER

O JESUS, mighty King, remember now that when thou wast plunged into the bitter waters of thy Passion until they closed over thy Head, thou wast forsaken not only by men but by thy Father also, and didst cry with a loud voice, saying: *My God, my God, why hast thou forsaken me?* By this thine anguish and dereliction, I beseech thee, forsake me not in my last agony. Amen.

EIGHTH PRAYER

O JESUS, strong Lion of the tribe of Juda, remember now the sorrow and the woe thou didst endure, when all the forces of thy

Heart and of thy Flesh failed thee utterly, and thou didst bow thy Head and cry: *It is consummated.* By this thine anguish and thy woe, have mercy on me at the end of my life, when my soul shall be troubled, and my spirit disquieted within me. Amen.

NINTH PRAYER

O JESUS, Splendour of the Father's glory and Figure of his substance, remember now that earnest commendation with which thou didst commend thy spirit to the Father, saying: *Father, into thy hands I commend my spirit!* and when, thy most sacred Body being torn and thy Heart broken, and all the bowels of thy compassion laid bare for our redemption, thou didst give up the ghost: I beseech thee by all that love which moved thee, the Life of all that live, to submit to die, that thou wouldest mortify and kill in my soul whatever is displeasing to thee. Amen.

TENTH PRAYER

O JESUS, true and fruitful Vine, remember now the lavish, the excessive profusion wherewith thou didst shed thy most Precious Blood, when on the cross thou didst tread the winepress alone, and wast crushed as a cluster of ripe grapes; when thou didst give us water and blood from thy pierced side, so that not one drop remained in thy Heart. Then wast thou hanged up as a bundle of myrrh, and thy tender Flesh grew pale, and thy moisture was all dried up within thee, and the marrow of thy bones consumed. By this thy most bitter Passion, and by the shedding of thy Most Precious Blood, I beseech thee, O most loving Jesus, wash my soul at the hour of my death with the water which flowed from thy Sacred Side, and adorn it with comeliness in the Precious Blood of thy sweetest Heart, and render it acceptable in thy sight in the fragrant odour of thy divine love. Amen.

OBLATION

O ACCEPT, O compassionate Jesus, this my prayer with that exceeding love wherewith thou didst endure a bitter death, and didst offer it, together with all the fruit of thy most sacred Humanity, to God the Father on the day of thine ascension: and by the depth of those wounds which scarred thy Flesh and pierced thy Hands and Feet and Heart, I beseech thee, raise me up, who am steeped and sunk in sin, and render me well-pleasing to thee in all things. Amen.

FIVE OFFERINGS OF THE PASSION OF CHRIST
FOR SINS

Our Lord said to St. Gertrude on one occasion: If you believe that I offered myself to God the Father on the cross, believe also that I now desire with the same love to be daily offered to God the Father for each sinner in particular; so that, however heavy be the load of sins beneath which a man feels himself oppressed, he may take comfort in the hope of pardon if he offer to God the Father my most spotless Passion and Death, and may be assured that he will reap abundant fruit of mercy and indulgence.

FIRST OFFERING

A LMIGHTY and eternal God, unfailing Fountain of mercy, who dost not despise those that come unto thee, notwithstanding their utter unworthiness, but dost cleanse them from their sins; behold, I, a vile sinner, weighed down beneath a grievous burden of sins, confess to thee in the spirit of humility and with a contrite heart, that I have been exceedingly ungrateful to thee my God, and have offended thee in manifold ways. But now I come to thee, and prostrate myself before thee with true contrition, and implore thy mercy. And as I have nothing of greater worth to offer thee in satisfaction for my sins than the most holy Life and Passion of thy Son, therefore I offer thee that surpassing love wherewith thy Only-begotten took on him our nature, and during three-and-thirty years endured so many toils and fatigues, so much anguish and woe, for our sake; and I make this offering to thee through the sweetest Heart of Jesus Christ, in the power of the Holy Ghost, and for all the sins which I have committed from my birth upwards even to this hour, with the full consent of my will and the delectation of my heart, I offer thee the apprehension and the sorrowfulness which he felt when he said: My soul is sorrowful, even unto death, I offer thee that sweat of blood which his impetuous love and his thrilling anguish wrung from his sacred Body, and that thrice-repeated prayer which he poured forth to thee from the midst of his Agony. I offer thee his ignominious bondage, his stripes and bruises, his insults and blasphemies, his blows and buffetings, the plucking out of his hair, and the spitting on his adorable face, which he endured in the houses of Annas and of Caiaphas in that same night; and setting forth all these before thee with gratitude and lively compassion. I beseech thine inexhaustible goodness that by their virtue and merit thou wouldst wash me from my sins, and render me in all things well-pleasing to thee. Amen.

After each of these offerings you may say a Pater noster.

SECOND OFFERING

O MOST compassionate God, for all the perverse and wicked actions which I have done with the several members of my body I offer thee that inexpressible affront and grief which thy Son endured, when his sacred Face was so shamefully spit upon and smitten; when he was unjustly accused before Pilate and Herod, was scornfully mocked and blasphemously insulted. 1 offer thee the ignominious stripping off of his garments, the harsh binding to the pillar, his painful scourging, his grievous wounds, and his excessive effusion of blood. Behold, O compassionate Father, with what composed modesty he stood at the pillar, how with all his heart he sighed unto thee, how many blows and gashes he received, and with how many wounds his flesh was torn, what anguish penetrated even to his bones, and how many the drops of his most sacred Blood which flowed forth from his wounds; and setting forth all these before thee, with gratitude and lively compassion, I beseech thee that by their virtue and their merit thou wouldst receive me into thy favour, and render me in all things well-pleasing to thee. Amen.

THIRD OFFERING

O MOST long-suffering God, for all the good I have omitted through my sloth and lukewarmness, I offer thee that love wherewith thy Son endured his intolerable anguish, when he was crowned with thorns, hailed with impious derision, shamefully spit upon, smitten with reeds and buffeted, dragged before the judgment-seat and unjustly condemned; when a murderer and thief was preferred to him, and an ungodly rabble clamoured for his death. I offer thee that way of sorrows he went to the Mount Calvary, laden with his heavy cross; I offer thee the weariness of his sacred limbs, the ruthlessness of the soldiers, the shouts and derision of the mob, his footprints traced in blood, and whatsoever he did or suffered throughout his whole life. And setting forth all these before thee with gratitude and lively compassion, I beseech thine inexhaustible goodness, that by their virtue and their merit thou wouldst wash me from my sins, and render me in all things well-pleasing to thee. Amen.

FOURTH OFFERING

O MOST merciful God, for all the sins and iniquities which I have committed against thee with my body or my soul, I offer thee all that exceeding sorrow which thy Son endured, when the garments which cleaved to his lacerated flesh were roughly stripped off, and all his wounds thus mercilessly torn open afresh. I offer thee the cruel and most fearful anguish of his Heart, when his most sacred Hands and Feet were nailed to the cross. Remember, O most compassionate Father, how humbly and how piteously thy Son laid himself down upon the cross, not knowing where to lay his head by reason of the intensity of his intolerable agony. Remember what tears

his eyes poured forth to thee, what sighs broke
forth from his heart towards thee, how many
drops of priceless blood dripped from his
sacred wounds, what sorrow and horror of
thick darkness pervaded his human soul as
death came slowly onwards. I set forth before
thee with gratitude and lively compassion all
these bloodsheddings and tears, all the anguish
of his distorted and dislocated limbs, all his
groanings and sighs, and all the love and the
patience with which thy Son endured them all;
beseeching thee that thou wouldst cleanse me
from my sins, and render me in all things well-
pleasing to thee. Amen.

FIFTH OFFERING

O MOST gracious and clement God, for all
my sins, mortal and venial, for all my
negligences and omissions, for all the guilt I
have contracted and all the punishment I have
deserved, I offer thee the unutterable anguish
which pierced the Heart of thy Son when the
cross was uplifted and let fall suddenly into
its place, and all the weight of his sacred Body
was borne by three nails. I offer to thee all the
scornful mockeries and the blasphemies which
assailed his sacred Ears, all the words he
uttered from the cross, all the tears he shed,
all the quivering of his holy limbs in their
agony, all the anguish and torment of his
sacred Heart, all the sighs and prayers which

he breathed towards thee, all his shrinking from nakedness and from the rude gaze of the crowd, all his acts of virtue on the cross, all the compassion, the sobs, the tears of his most desolate Mother and of all his friends; I offer thee, last of all, that most bitter, most cruel, most agonising death, which impetuous love and thrilling anguish inflicted on him, most humbly beseeching thee that, by the merits of his most holy Life and Passion and Death, thou wouldst wash my soul from all its stains and defilements in his most precious Blood, and adorn it with the merits and virtues of his Humanity, and strengthen it at its departure hence with his Passion and his Death. Amen.

THE VICTIM OF SIN

A prayer in which our Blessed Lord hanging on the cross is offered to God the Father.

LOOK down, O pitiful Father, from the throne of thy Majesty and the lofty habitation of thy heavens, and behold thy beloved Son hanging so piteously and so ignominiously on the cross, his sacred Body all stretched, and racked, and torn with cruel wounds. Look down upon that spotless Lamb, who opened not his mouth when in the jaws of the wolves, to speak one word of deprecation or complaint. See thy most beloved Son, thy sweet Jesus, shedding his Blood with such profuse liberality for the sin of his brethren. Behold that sacred Head, before which the Powers of heaven bow in reverent awe, now itself bowed in dereliction and in anguish. See that Face, fairer than the sons of men, defiled with spittings, seamed with scars, besmeared with blood, and marred with livid bruises. Behold his eyes swimming in tears, his gracious mouth distorted, his sunken pallid cheeks, his hair plucked off, his arms so painfully stretched, his bones out of joint, his breast torn with wounds, his skin all scarred with gashes, his weak and trembling knees, his hands and feet dug through with cruel nails, his pierced side, his heart laid open, and all his limbs swollen with scourging and with blows. Remember, O most compassionate Father, who it is that suffers; and remember in thy mercy for whom he suffers. Is not this thy well-beloved Son, whom thou hast begotten from everlasting, and cherished in thine inmost heart? Is not this that most spotless Lamb who, obedient to thee even unto death, hath offered himself a sacrifice and a victim for our sins? Suffer thyself, then, to be touched with that great sight which thine only-begotten Son hath set before thee upon the cross, and with the satisfaction he hath made for our sins. Remember all his groanings, remember all the tears he shed upon the cross, while he prayed for those who had crucified him, saying: Father, forgive them! To this end I set forth before thee and offer thee, for my innumerable sins, offences, and negligences, this thy Son, who is made unto me justice, and sanctification, and redemption. Behold, O most holy Father, I set before thee thy most humble Son, who has made most abundant atonement to thee for all my sins of pride. I set forth before thee and offer thee this thy most meek and gentle Son, who has made atonement to thee for all my sins of anger. I offer thee thy most loving Son, who has fully satisfied for all my sins of hatred. His most gracious liberality has paid whatever debt I have contracted through my avarice. His most holy works have made amends for my sloth. His most perfect abstinence has satisfied for my gluttony. The purity of his most holy life has blotted out whatever sins I have ever committed by evil thoughts, or words, or deeds. His entire and finished obedience, wherein he was obedient unto thee even unto death, has effaced my disobedience. Lastly, let his universal and absolute perfection plead for my utter imperfection and lack of all virtues. This is my treasure, O most compassionate Father, in which I put my trust; this is the price wherewith I pay thee all my debts. I beseech thee, therefore, by the virtue of all the prayers which thy Son poured out before thee on behalf of sinners, that thou wouldst deign to render this my oblation valid, acceptable, and availing; and by the most sinless Humanity of the same Jesus Christ thy Son to look on me as pure and cleansed from all sin, and endowed and adorned by his glorious Divinity with all those virtues wherewith that same Divinity caused his most holy Humanity to blossom and to bear fruit. Amen.

A SHORTER OFFERING

This prayer was revealed to St. Gertrude during a marvellous and unusual visitation of grace, and she was told at the same time that our Lord would accept it with singular favour from all who repeated it. It became so familiar to the saint that during her last illness she repeated it continually.

O MOST loving Father, in atonement and satisfaction for all my sins, I offer thee all the whole Passion of thy most beloved Son, from the plaintive wail he uttered when laid upon straw in the manger, through all the helplessness of his infancy, the privations of his boyhood, the adversities of his youth, the sufferings of his manhood, until that hour when he bowed his Head upon the cross with a loud cry, and gave up the ghost. And, in atonement and satisfaction for all my negligences, I offer thee, O most loving Father, all the whole most holy life and conversation of thy Son, most perfect in its every thought, and word, and action, from the hour when he came down from his lofty throne to the Virgin's womb, and thence came forth into our dreary wilderness, to the hour when he presented to thy

Fatherly regard the glory of his conquering Flesh. Amen.

PRAYER TO JESUS SUFFERING

This prayer was very familiar to St. Gertrude, and through its use she obtained the great grace that the stigmata of the Most Sacred Wounds of our Lord were impressed upon her heart.

O LORD Jesus Christ, Son of the living God, grant that I may aspire towards thee with all my heart, with yearning desire, with a soul ever athirst for thee; that I may breathe in thee alone, who art all sweetness and all delight; and that my whole spirit and my inmost heart may pant for thee, their true blessedness. O most merciful Lord, engrave thy Wounds upon my heart with thy most precious Blood, that I may read in them all thy grief and all thy love; and may the memory of thy Wounds ever abide in the secret of my heart, to excite my most lively compassion and to enkindle my most glowing love. Grant also that all creatures may grow vile in my eyes, and be thou alone sweet to my heart. Amen.

ASPIRATION OF A SOUL CONDOLING WITH JESUS IN HIS PASSION

Our Lord said to St. Mechtilde: Whenever any one sighs towards me with love in meditat-

ing on my Passion, it is as though he gently touched my Wounds with a fresh-budding rose, and I wound his heart in return with the arrow of my love. Moreover, if he shed tears of devotion over my Passion, I will accept them as though he had suffered for me. And how shall I obtain this gift of tears? asked the saint. Then our Lord taught her the following prayer:

O MOST tender Jesus who didst come to seek and to save that which was lost; alas, how cruelly and how unworthily has the world treated thee, and how black has been its ingratitude to thee, who didst lay down thy beloved soul for its salvation! I condole with thee, O my most loving Brother, and 1 compassionate thee from my inmost heart, when I call to mind the mournful desolation in which thou, most faithful of friends, wast left by all thy friends; how thou wast ruthlessly seized as a thief and a robber, and cruelly bound, and driven towards thy death, scornfully mocked by thine enemies, and assailed with insults and outrages; and didst become as a worm and no man, the reproach of men, and the outcast of the people. Who can meditate without tears on the loving gentleness with which thou wentest forth to meet thine enemies, as they came with swords and with staves to seize thee and deliver thee to death, even as a tender mother goes forth to meet the son of her love; and how thou didst meekly resign thyself into their cruel hands, to rescue them from the jaws of the wolves of hell! While they so pitilessly smote thee, for every blow and for every buffeting thou didst impress a kiss of love on all the souls which should be saved through thy Passion until the day of doom. O, how great was thy love towards thine enemies, O most tender Jesus, in that, even while they were cruelly scourging thee, thou didst pour forth for them such availing prayer, that many of them were converted unto thee! And when they thrust the crown of thorns on thy most sacred Head, thou didst weave into their crowns as many gems as there were thorns in thine own. O most gentle Jesus, who can think without an ardent love of thee on the amazing love thou didst manifest towards us most ungrateful sinners, when thy sinless hands and feet were so inhumanly nailed to the cross, and all thy limbs so painfully stretched and dragged asunder that all thy bones might be numbered; and thou, the while, wast drawing towards thee, with all the might of thy Divinity, the souls of as many as were ordained to life everlasting. And when thy sacred Side was opened with the lance, thou didst offer the cup of life, filled from thine own Heart, to all who had drunk in Adam the cup of death, that in thee, who art the Life, all might be made sons of everlasting life and blessedness. Wherefore, O thou tenderest Lover of my soul, in return for thy love, and for the undeserved bitterness of thy guiltless Passion, I offer thee my whole heart, earnestly desiring, from this moment to the time of my departure hence, to bear with thee all the bitterness and the sorrow of thy sweetest Heart, and of thine immaculate Body; and beseeching thee to wound my heart with a sense and sympathy in thy Passion, and evermore to keep alive its memory within me. Amen.

PRAYER TO JESUS SUFFERING

Our Lord said to St. Mechtilde: Behold, I make over to thee all the bitterness of my Passion, that thou mayest offer it to me again as though it were thine own possession. And whoever shall do this shall receive double at my hand, and whenever he renews this offering he shall assuredly receive the double; and this is that hundredfold which a man receives in this life, and in the world to come life everlasting.

O MOST gracious Jesus, Redeemer and Saviour of the whole human race, I recall to thy mind with gratitude and love all the sorrow and anxiety which thou, my Creator and my God, didst feel in thine Agony, when thou didst pray yet longer, and didst bedew the earth with the sweat of Blood, wrung from thee by thine exceeding anguish, desire, and love; beseeching thee by all and each of those most sacred drops, all which I

here offer thee with devout affection, that thou
wouldest wash away all the stains of my sins.
I recall to thy mind thy being unjustly bound
with heavy chains, thy innumerable stripes and
blows, and all the contumely and the blasphemy wherewith thou wast assailed, when all
proclaimed thee a deceiver of the people; when
thou wast falsely accused before Pilate, ignominiously mocked by Herod, and set aside
for an impious robber; and when all the whole
multitude clamorously demanded that thou
shouldst be crucified. And all this thou didst
endure with such love and such patience that
although thou couldst by one look have ap-
palled thine adversaries, and with one word
convicted the false witnesses against thee, yet
thou didst submit to be led as a sheep to the
slaughter, and stand before thy judge with thy
head bowed in humility, thine eyes fixed on the
ground, not once opening thy mouth to speak
one word of complaint at the lying accusations
brought against thee.   Wherefore I give thee
thanks on behalf of all mankind, and offer
thee all the outrages and the insults heaped
on thee, in satisfaction for all the insult I have
done thee by my sins. I give thee thanks also,
and I recall to thy mind thy most cruel and
excessive scourging, wherein thy whole Body
was so gashed and torn that from the sole of
thy foot to the top of thy head there was no
soundness in thee. I set forth now before thee,

likewise, that intolerable agony thou didst feel when the crown of thorns was so harshly forced upon thy kingly Head, when the sharp thorns pierced thy head and thy brow, and were thrust even into thy brain, and thy most gentle loving face, into which the Angels desire to look, was covered with slow-trickling drops of thy roseate Blood. O most pitiful Jesus, I now recall to thy mind the unutterable anguish which thrilled through thy whole Body when thou wast fastened to the cross with iron nails, when thou wast lifted up on high on thy cross, and blasphemed by the Jews, mocked in thy thirst with vinegar and gall, and hung up between two robbers as the refuse and offscouring of all creatures. Lastly, O most gracious Jesus, I recall to thy mind with gratitude and compassion all and each of the sorrows thou didst feel throughout thy whole most sacred Body, and especially in thy sweetest Heart, by reason of thy fore-knowledge that thy most bitter, thy most shameful, most guiltless Passion would be of no avail to so many. And then thy deified Heart itself broke with excessive love and grief, and thy most holy Soul quitted thy blessed Body with an inconceivable pang! For all these thy sorrows I give thee infinite thanks; and through thy sweetest Heart, in the power of the Holy Ghost, and on behalf of and with the love of all creatures, 1 offer thee all thy grief, and pain, and torment of body and of soul, throughout all the time of thy Passion, for all the sins 1 have committed, for all the good I have left undone or done negligently, and to turn away all the punishment I have so justly deserved. Do thou now vouchsafe to ratify and accept this my oblation, and to absolve me from all my sins. Amen.

SALUTATION OF ALL THE SACRED LIMBS OF JESUS

In obedience to a divine inspiration, St. Gertrude was wont to salute each member of our Lord which had suffered in his Passion; whenever she did so, a divine splendour appeared to emanate from the sacred members thus 'saluted, and to irradiate her whole soul. In that splendour she was clothed with that innocence which our Lord acquired for us by the sufferings of that particular member. Wherefore let us not neglect this holy practice, if we would have some part in this blessing.

HAIL, tender Limbs of my Lord Jesus Christ, tormented in thy Passion with manifold pain for our salvation. Hail, thou adorable Head, crowned for us with thorns, and stricken with the reed. Hail, most worshipful Face, for us spit upon and smitten. Hail, most gentle Eyes of our Saviour, for us suffused with tears. Hail, sacred Mouth, filled for us with vinegar and gall. Hail, most noble Ears, pierced for us with reproach and contumely. Hail, thou kingly Neck, buffeted for us; and most holy Back, for us torn with the scourge. Hail, venerable Hands and Arms, stretched out for us upon the cross. Hail, divine Breast, disquieted for us, and mangled in the Passion. Hail, adorable Knees, bent in prayer for us, now crushed and out of joint. Hail, most worshipful Feet, pierced for us with the nails. Hail, glorious Side, riven for us with the soldier's lance. Hail, whole Body of my Jesus, hanged for us on the cross, torn and wounded, dead and buried. Hail, sacred Heart, dropping like the honeycomb, treasure-house of the most Blessed Trinity, broken for us on the cross. Hail, thrice-holy Soul of Jesus Christ, sorrowful for us even unto death. Hail, most precious Blood, flowing so lavishly from the wounds of Jesus. Hail, adorable Wounds of my Saviour, tokens of his love and price of our redemption, inflicted on Jesus in his Passion, and now radiant as stars in the highest heaven. O, write my name in these thy Wounds, good Jesus, and hide me therein from the face of the tempter. And by the many wounds and merits of all thy sacred Limbs, vouchsafe to my soul at its departure hence that innocence which thou hast acquired for thy Church by their several anguish and passion. Amen.

PRAYER TO JESUS HANGING ON THE CROSS

O MY most dear and loving Lord Jesus
Christ, by the unutterable love wherewith
thou didst love the race of men, when thou,
the King of Heaven, didst hang upon the
cross, thy Body all marred with wounds, thy
Heart pierced through, thy Senses confused,
thy most beauteous Face so piteously sad, thy
ruddy Wounds dripping blood, thine Arms
stretched out and thy Feet dug through, thy
most sacred Limbs all wrenched and out of
joint, thy Mouth livid and thy Countenance
pale, thy tearful Eyes dimmed with the shadow
of death, thy Breast heaving with sighs, thy
Head bowed, thy Side laid open, and thy Soul
saturated with sorrows: by all these, and by
the love which broke thy sweetest Heart when
thy blessed Soul went forth from thy Body,
have mercy on my soul, I beseech thee, in the
hour of my going hence. Amen.

THREE THANKSGIVINGS TO JESUS ON THE CROSS

*St. Mechtilde once asked our Lord, in prayer,
which had been his greatest suffering. Our
Lord replied: The being so forcibly stretched
out upon the cross that all my bones might
have been numbered; and if any one give me
special thanks for that suffering, it shall be as
though he anointed my wounds with fragrant
ointment. And if any one give me thanks for*

the thirst I suffered, it shall be as though he had allayed that thirst in my Passion; moreover, if he give me thanks that I willed to be fastened to my cross with nails, he shall be as acceptable to me as though he had taken me down from it.

O MOST meek and gentle Lamb of God, who during three long hours didst hang so piteously upon the cross; with the affection of all thy creatures I give thee thanks for that intolerable pain thou didst endure when thou wast so cruelly stretched out upon thy sacred cross that all thy bones might be numbered: beseeching thee by that pain to forgive me all the sins which I have ever committed against thee with any member of my body. Amen.

O MOST innocent Lamb of God, with the gratitude of every creature of thy hands I give thee thanks for the bitter thirst thou didst suffer for the salvation of the world, when with plaintive voice thou didst exclaim: *I thirst;* and when nothing was given thee to drink but only vinegar and gall; beseeching thee by the bitterness of that thirst to forgive me all the sins which I have ever committed against thee by immoderate eating and drinking. Amen.

O MOST sacred Lamb of God, with the mutual gratitude of the Three Persons of the One adorable Trinity I give thee thanks for all

the dread anguish thou didst endure when
thou wast so pitilessly fastened to the cross
with iron nails driven through thy sacred Hands
and Feet; so that thy heart shuddered and thy
whole frame quivered with agony. By this thy
strong pain and thy most bitter death, I beseech thee to wash away the sins of my hands
and my feet, and to appease thy Father's wrath
against me by showing thy most sacred Wounds
for me. Amen.

PRAISE TO JESUS DESPISED IN HIS PASSION

Taught to St. Mechtilde by our Lord himself.

O JESUS, most glorious in thy magnificence, I praise and bless thine incomprehensible omnipotence, thus weak and helpless
for us in thy Passion. I adore and glorify thine
unsearchable wisdom, thus accounted foolish-
ness for us. I praise and magnify thine unutterable love, which did submit to be hated of all
men for the sake of thine elect. I praise and
extol thy meek and gentle mercy, sentenced to
so fearful a death for us men. I praise and
adore thy ravishing sweetness, embittered for
us by thy most bitter death. Amen.

LOVING AFFECTIONS TO JESUS BLASPHEMED IN HIS PASSION

*When St. Gertrude heard, in the Gospel of the
Mass the words:* Thou hast a devil; *she was*

*unutterably distressed at so blasphemous a re-
proach, and addressed to our Lord the following prayer. While she was repeating it with
most tender affection, our Lord appeared to
draw near to her and to greet her, saying:
Whoever shall salute me with the like affection
in reparation for the blasphemies heaped upon
me, in the dreadful day of judgment I will
show him such tender affection in return, that
all his adversaries shall be amazed and flee
away.*

HAIL, life-giving Germ of divine Majesty!
hail, unfading Flower of human dignity!
O most loving Jesus, for all the blasphemies
and contumely with which thou wast assailed
on earth, I salute and bless thee with all the
affection and love of the whole creation. For
every drop of thy Precious Blood shed in thy
Passion, for every Wound thou didst bear in
thy sacred Body, for every blow and stripe and
bruise, I salute and bless thee ten thousand
fold. For every tear thou didst shed, for every
sigh thou didst breathe forth, for every sorrow
thou didst feel, I bless and salute thee, O my
sweetest Jesus, ten thousand fold. For every
act of virtue thou didst do, for every thirsting
desire with which thou didst yearn for our
salvation, for every look of love thou didst
bend on thy Mother and thy friends, I bless
and salute thee ten thousand fold. For every
fall along thy way of sorrows, for every

shrinking and sinking of thy Human Flesh, for every movement of thy sacred Hands and Feet, I salute and bless thee ten thousand fold. I bless and salute thee ten thousand times, O meekest Jesus, for every drop of Blood that fell to the ground in thy sweat of agony, for every painful step of thy weary Feet, for every strong cry and tear wherewith thou didst offer thy prayers and thy supplication to thy Father. I salute and bless thee ten thousand times, O most gentle Jesus, for every gash with which thy sacred Body was torn in thy scourging, for every thorn of thy cruel crown which entered into thy Flesh, for all the loathsome spittings with which thou wast defiled. I bless and salute thee ten thousand times for every cord with which thou wast bound, for every reproach and outrage wherewith thy soul was saturated, for every impious greeting of scorn with which thou wast insulted. For every false charge brought against thee, O sinless Jesus, for every foul and impious lie uttered in disparagement of thee, and for every unjust sentence pronounced upon thee, I bless and salute thee ten thousand fold. Would, O most gracious Jesus, that I could multiply these my salutations and praises ten thousand times ten thousand fold, and offer them to thee every hour of my life; that so I might efface and make amends for all the insults, the contumely, and the blasphemy hurled against thee, my sweetest Redeemer! I pray thee, despise not the desire nor the sighing of thy poor, but, according to thine own essential goodness, deign to ratify and accept them. Amen.

SALUTATION OF THE WOUND IN THE SIDE

(*St. Mechtilde and St. Gertrude*)

O LORD Jesus, compassionate Pelican, who hast cleansed us unclean in thine own Blood, I give thee thanks for the sweet and adorable Wound of love which thou didst receive on the cross, when thine all-conquering love opened thy sweet-flowing Side, and wounded thy most sacred Heart with an arrow of love. Blessed for ever be that life-giving stroke and that most hallowed Wound; and blessed be the adorable Blood, and the water of salvation which gushed forth from it, to wash away all our sins! Wash me, unclean, O compassionate Jesus, in that cleansing water, anoint my feeble soul, and quicken it with that sacred Blood; and grant that at my last hour my portion and heritage may be but one drop of that divine stream. O most loving Jesus, by thy pierced Heart, I pray thee, wound my heart with that arrow of love; so that nothing of earth may abide in it more, but that it be filled with thy glowing love alone for ever. Amen.

SALUTATION OF THE WOUND IN THE SHOULDER
OF JESUS

It is related in the annals of Clairvaux that St. Bernard once asked our Lord which was his greatest unrecorded suffering, and that our Lord condescended to answer: I had on my shoulder, while I bore my cross on the way of sorrows, a most grievous wound, which was more painful to me than the others, and which is not recorded by men because they knew not of it. Honour this wound with thy devotion, and I will grant thee whatsoever thou dost ask through its virtue and merit. And in regard of all those who shall venerate this wound, I will remit to them all their venial sins, and will no more remember their mortal sins.

O MOST loving Jesus, meekest Lamb of God, I, a miserable sinner, salute and worship the most sacred Wound of the shoulder on which thou didst bear thy heavy cross, which so tore thy Flesh and laid bare thy Bones as to inflict on thee an anguish greater than any other wound of thy most blessed Body. I adore thee, O Jesus most sorrowful; I praise thee, I bless and glorify thee, and give thee thanks for this most sacred and most painful Wound; beseeching thee, by that exceeding pain, and by the crushing burden of thy heavy cross, to be merciful to me a sinner, to forgive me all my mortal and all my venial sins, and to lead me on towards heaven along the way of thy cross. Amen.

LITANY OF THE PASSION

L ORD have mercy.
Christ have mercy.
Lord have mercy.
Jesus hear us.
Jesus graciously hear us.
O God the Father, of heaven,
O God the Son, Redeemer of the world,
O God the Holy Ghost,
Holy Trinity, one God,
Jesus, Son of the living God,
By thy most holy life and conversation,
By thy most bitter passion and death,
By thy sorrow and thine agony in the garden,
By thy thrice-repeated prayer,
By thy resignation of thy human will,
By thy sweat of Blood,
By thy harsh captivity,
By thy bonds and stripes,
By thy sacred Body buffeted and smitten,
By thy mockings and thine ignominy,
By the spitting upon thy adorable Face,
By the false judgment pronounced on thee by Caiaphas,
By thy setting at naught by Herod,
By the shameful stripping off thy garments,
By thy cruel scourging,
By thy painful crown of thorns,
By thy purple robe,
By thy most unjust condemnation,

Have mercy on us.

By thy bearing thine own cross,

By thy footprints traced in blood,

By the wound in thy sacred shoulder,

By the tearing off thy garments,

By the cruel stretching of all thy sacred limbs,

By thy dread crucifixion,

By the upraising of thy cross,

By the taunts and blasphemies of thine enemies,

By thy seven words and thy thirst,

By the compassion of thy Mother,

By the woe of all thy friends,

By the anguish of thy Heart and of thy Body,

By thy tears and prayers,

By the dropping of thy most precious Blood,

By thy patience and humility,

By the love of thy sweetest Heart,

By the love wherewith thou didst pray for sinners,

By the love wherewith thou didst endure all thy torments and sorrows,

By the love wherewith thou didst will to die a cruel death,

By the love wherewith thou didst will thy sacred Side to be opened with the lance,

By the love wherewith thou didst will to be laid in the sepulchre,

By the most acceptable sacrifice which

Have mercy on us.

thou didst offer to thy Father in thy Passion,

By the intercession of thy dearest Mother and of all thine elect,

By thine infinite dignity and worth,

Lamb of God, who takest away the sins of the world,

Spare us, O Lord.

Lamb of God, who takest away the sins of the world,

Graciously hear us, O Lord.

Lamb of God, who takest away the sins of the world,

Have mercy on us.

Jesus, hear us.

Jesus, graciously hear us.

Ant. O Saviour of the world, save us, who by thy cross and blood hast redeemed us; grant us thine aid, we beseech thee, O our God.

V. We adore thee, O Christ, and we bless thee.

R. Because by thy cross thou hast redeemed the world.

Let us pray

O LORD Jesus Christ, Son of the living God, who didst at the sixth hour go up on the cross for the redemption of the world, and shed thy blood for the remission of our sins; we humbly beseech thee that by the virtue and merits of thy most holy life, passion, and death, thou wouldst grant us to enter into the gates of Paradise with joy, who livest, &c.

Have mercy on us.

PART VI

TO THE BLESSED VIRGIN MARY

OFFICE OF B.V.M.

St. Gertrude said to our Lord: Teach me, O my Lord, how I may show my devotion and love to thy blessed Mother, since I am unable to recite her office. Then our Lord taught her the following prayers; and when she recited them she seemed to see him offering his divine Heart in likeness of a vessel of gold, of which, when she had drunk, she appeared filled with gladness. Hence she learned that whenever these prayers are recited, our Lord thus presents his Heart to the lips of his blessed Mother, and that in the fulness of her maternal delight she graciously rewards those who recite them.

AT MATINS

O MOST compassionate Jesus, I praise thee with the tuneful praise which thine own sweetest Heart gives forth, for the innocence of that most spotless virginity whereby thy peerless and ever-blessed Mother was a Virgin in her conception of thee, a Virgin when she brought thee forth, and ever remained a Virgin most inviolate after thy sacred birth; imitating thus thine own innocence, when in the early dawn thou wast seized and bound for the redemption of our captive race, and buffeted and smitten, and cruelly and piteously assailed with contumely and manifold reproach.

The following prayer should be said at all the Hours:

O MOTHER of all blessedness, peerless sanctuary of the Holy Ghost, I praise and greet thee through the sweetest Heart of Jesus Christ, the Son of God and thy most loving Son; beseeching thee to succour us in all our needs and distresses, and at the hour of our death. Amen.

AT PRIME

I PRAISE thee, O most compassionate Jesus, through thine own sweetest Heart, for that placid deep humility whereby the Virgin undefiled became day by day more fitted and more worthy to conceive thee; imitating thus thy humility, when thou, who wilt come to be the Judge of the living and the dead, didst at the first hour of the day condescend to be judged by a Gentile and an alien, for the redemption of the human race.

O Mother of all blessedness, &c.

AT TIERCE

I PRAISE thee, O most compassionate Jesus, through thine own sweetest Heart, for that most ardent yearning desire whereby the Virgin full of pity drew thee, the Son of God, from the bosom of the eternal Father into her most pure womb; imitating thus that most impetuous desire wherewith thou didst desire our salvation, when thou wast scourged with cruel thongs and crowned with thorns, and didst condescend at the third hour of the day to bear thy cross of ignominy on thy wearied bleeding shoulder with uncomplaining meekness and patience.

O Mother of all blessedness, &c.

AT SEXT

I PRAISE thee, O most compassionate Jesus, through thine own sweetest Heart, for that steadfast and undismayed hope wherewith the heavenly Virgin strove unceasingly, with fixed will and holy intention, to praise thee; imitating thus that eager yearning wherewith, when hanging high on the tree of thy cross, and amid the exceeding bitterness of thy death, thou didst long with all thy whole soul for the redemption of the human race, and didst therefore cry: *I thirst.* For what didst thou thirst, O loving Jesus, but for the salvation of the souls of men, for which thou wouldst have joyfully endured yet more bitter and consuming anguish.

O Mother of all blessedness, &c.

AT NONE

I PRAISE thee, O most compassionate Jesus, through thine own sweetest Heart, for that most ardent mutual love which united thy divine Heart to that of the Virgin undefiled, and which most intimately and inseparably conjoined thy all-glorious Divinity with thy Humanity in her most pure womb; so that it was thus given her to imitate thee in the exceeding greatness of thy love; thou, the Life of all that live who didst at the ninth hour bow thy head in bitterest death upon the cross for our redemption.

O Mother of all blessedness, &c.

AT VESPERS

I PRAISE thee, O most compassionate Jesus, through thine own sweetest Heart, for that most firm and rooted faith whereby the blessed Virgin stood alone, unshrinking, beneath the cross, when thine Apostles had forsaken thee, and all had fled in dismay; imitating thus thy faithfulness in death, when thou didst go in quest of thine own even into Limbus, and drawing them thence, with the strong right hand of thy mercy, didst bear them up to the joys of thy Paradise.

O Mother of all blessedness, &c.

AT COMPLINE

I PRAISE thee, O most compassionate Jesus, through thine own sweetest Heart, for the incomparable perseverance wherewith thy most-blessed Mother persevered in virtue and in good works even to the end; imitating thus thine unresting, unwearying zeal in the work of our redemption, when, having obtained for us by thy most bitter death, thou didst not shrink from giving thine incorruptible Body to the grave, after the manner of men; that thou mightest show us that there was no depth of humiliation from which thy love would shrink, in order to effect our complete salvation.

O Mother of all blessedness, &c.

ACT OF REPARATION

Most pleasing to the blessed Virgin

While St. Gertrude was bewailing her negligence in that she had never served the Mother of Jesus with due reverence, and was beseeching our Lord to supply her lack of service, she seemed to see the King of Glory arise and present his deific Heart to his Mother, and therewith to make amends for all her negligence. To obtain a like grace, recite the following prayer:

O SWEETEST Jesus, by that love where-with thou didst deign to take our flesh of the most pure Virgin and of her to be born, that thou mightest satisfy the desires of the poor and the wants of the needy, I beseech thee that thou wouldst vouchsafe to make amends to thy ever-virgin Mother, with thine own sweetest Heart, for all the manifold defects which through my own negligence and ingratitude have tainted and marred my service and honour of so gentle and loving a Mother, whose gracious succour has never failed me in any danger or necessity. Do thou, O most tender Jesus, present to her thy sweetest Heart, overflowing with ineffable blessedness, in reparation of this my neglect. Let her see therein all the divine love whereby thou didst from all eternity freely elect her to be thy Mother, didst preserve her from all taint of original sin, and incomparably adorn her with all graces and all virtues. Let her see therein all the tenderness wherewith thou didst cling to her when she cherished thee, her Child, in her bosom; all the constant unfailing love with which, during the whole time of thy sojourn on earth, thou, who art the Ruler of heaven and of earth, didst obey her as a son his mother; and especially in the hour of thy death, when, as though forgetting thine own intolerable anguish, and touched to the heart by her desolation, thou didst provide for her a guardian and a son. Let her see therein that

love beyond thought with which thou didst
show her how precious she is in thy sight,
when on the day of her most joyous Assumption thou didst exalt her high above all the
choirs of angels, and crown her Lady and
Queen of heaven and earth. And thus, O good
Jesus, may she be still to me a loving and
long-suffering Mother, and both in life and in
death my compassionate advocate and most
gracious patroness. Amen.

THANKSGIVING FOR THE GRACES BESTOWED ON THE BLESSED VIRGIN

*When St. Gertrude had recited this short
prayer, she saw in vision the Mother of divine
grace arise and beseech the Blessed Trinity to
grant her as large a measure of grace as the
heart of man can receive in this life. Then the
most glorious Trinity turned towards the saint,
and filled her soul with unutterable grace and
benediction.*

BLESSED be the ineffable, ever-adorable omnipotence of God the Father; and blessed
the wondrous and manifold wisdom of God
the Son; and blessed the amazing and most
tender goodness of the Holy Ghost, the
Paraclete; for that the ever-glorious Trinity
hath deigned to decree from eternity, to create
in time, and to bestow on us as our most
effectual help and succour, the Virgin so full
of all grace, in order that he might communi-

cate to her his own divine and superabounding beatitude. Amen.

GOLDEN SALUTATION OF THE BLESSED VIRGIN

The Blessed Virgin revealed to St. Gertrude that she rejoiced to show to those who thus saluted her the inestimable treasures of her loving compassion. And at the hour of his departure, she added, I will appear to him clothed with radiant beauty, and will pour into his soul heavenly sweetness and consolation.

HAIL, fair Lily of the effulgent and ever-peaceful Trinity. Hail, thou radiant Rose of heavenly fragrance, of whom the King of heaven did will to be born, and with thy milk to be fed: feed our souls with divine infusions. Amen.

HEAVENLY AVE MARIA

Which our Lord himself put in the mouth of St. Mechtilde.

HAIL, thou peerless offspring of the omnipotence of the Father, of the wisdom of the Son, and of the enrapturing goodness of the Holy Ghost, Mary, who dost fill heaven and earth with thy gentle light. Thou that art full of grace, the Lord is with thee, even the only-begotten Son of the Father, and the one only Son of the love of thy virgin heart, thy sweetest Spouse and thy Beloved. Blessed art

thou amongst women, for thou hast annulled
the curse of Eve, and hast brought back an
everlasting blessing. And blessed is the Fruit of
thy womb, Jesus Christ, the Lord and Creator
of all things, who doth evermore bless and
sanctify, enrich and quicken all things. Amen.

GOLDEN AVE MARIA

*While St. Mechtilde was ardently desiring to
greet the Blessed Virgin with the most sublime
salutation possible, she saw in vision our Lady,
bearing on her heart the angelical salutation
written in letters of gold, and saying to her:
No salutation can surpass this, nor can any be
so sweet in my ears as that with which God
the everlasting Father greeted me, in the following manner:*

HAIL, Mary, in union with that reverence
wherewith God the Father greeted thee
with *Ave,* and by his omnipotence delivered
thee from every woe and *Voe* of sin. Hail,
Mary, in union with that love wherewith the
Son of God enlightened thee with his wisdom,
and made thee a softly-shining star, lighting up
heaven and earth. Hail, Mary, in union with
that sweet unction of the Holy Ghost, wherewith he so pervaded thee and made thee so
full of grace, that every one who through thee
seeketh grace doth find it. Call to mind now
that unspeakable operation wherewith the
whole most Blessed Trinity wrought in thee,

when human flesh taken from thy substance was so united to the Divine Nature that God was made man and man became God, and thy whole soul was suffused with a sweetness and a gladness which the heart of man cannot conceive. And therefore every creature with rapturous admiration doth acknowledge and confess that thou art blessed and incomparably exalted above all creatures in heaven or on earth, and blessed the Fruit of thy womb, even Jesus, who quickens, sanctifies, and blesses all things for ever. Amen.

ACT OF JOY IN THE IMMACULATE CONCEPTION

To which Innocent VIII. attached an Indulgence at the request of the Queen of Spain.

HAIL, glorious Virgin, Morning-star that dost outshine the sun, gracious Mother of my God, sweeter than the dropping honeycomb: thou art that fair one in comparison with whom all beauty is pale and dim; thou art redder than the rose and more dazzling white than the lily; all virtues adorn thee, thou purer than the seraphim; and every saint doth give thee honour, thou that hast thy higher throne in the heavens. Amen.

THREE EFFICACIOUS PETITIONS TO THE BLESSED VIRGIN

When St. Gertrude recited these three petitions, which she had learned of the Blessed Virgin, it seemed to her as though she were so clothed and adorned with her surpassing merits, that the Lord of Majesty took ineffable delight in her.

O MOST blessed Virgin Mary, I beseech thee by the most spotless purity wherewith thou didst prepare in thy womb a still and glad abode for the Son of God, that by thy intercessions I may be cleansed from every stain.

O most blessed Virgin Mary, I beseech thee by that thy most gentle, deep humility whereby thou didst merit to be raised high above all angels and saints, that by thy intercessions all my negligences may be forgiven and satisfied for.

O most blessed Virgin Mary, I implore thee by that unutterable love which united thee inseparably to God, that by thy intercessions I may receive an abundance of all merit. Amen.

THE FIVE JOYS OF THE BLESSED VIRGIN

On one occasion, while St. Mechtilde was reflecting in sadness that she had never been duly devout to the Blessed Virgin, and was beseeching our Lord to teach her how to supply her defect, it seemed to her that our Lord bade her apply her lips to the wound in his side, saying: Draw hence that which thou dost wish to offer to my Mother. And she felt the five following salutations, which she had never heard or conceived before, trickle down upon her lips as so many drops of water.

I SALUTE thee, O Virgin most resplendent in glory, in that sweetest stream which flowed forth upon thee from the Heart of the most Holy Trinity, by reason of thy most blessed predestination from eternity.

I salute thee, O Virgin most radiant in holiness, in that sweetest stream which went forth upon thee from the Heart of the most Holy Trinity, by reason of thy most blessed conversation and life.

I salute thee, O Virgin, most noble, in that sweetest stream which shed itself forth upon thee from the Heart of the most Holy Trinity, through the teaching and preaching of thy Son.

I salute thee, O Virgin most full of love, in that sweetest stream which gushed forth upon thee from the Heart of the most Holy Trinity, through the bitter Passion and Death of thy Son.

I salute thee, O Virgin most worshipful, in that sweetest stream which burst forth upon thee from the Heart of the most Holy Trinity, and filled thee with all the glory, all the dazzling magnificence, and the ecstatic joy in which thou dost now exult, as beseemeth thee, the elect above and over all creatures before the world was formed. Amen.

AT THE ECCE ANCILLA DOMINI

Our blessed Lady said to St. Gertrude: Who-
ever shall devoutly recall to my mind the joy
which I felt in uttering the words: Behold the

handmaid of the Lord, *I will most truly show him that I am his Mother, and will unfailingly succour him.*

O MOTHER of blessedness and most august Sanctuary of the Holy Ghost, I praise and greet thee, and with most devout intention of mind recall to thee that unspeakable joy which thou didst feel when with calmest trustfulness thou didst commend to the divine Will thy whole unreserved self, and all that was to be done to thee and in thee, saying: *Behold the handmaid of the Lord:* beseeching thee that thou wouldst show thyself my Mother, and evermore succour me with the saving help of thy compassionate heart. Amen.

OFFERING OF THE HEART OF JESUS TO THE BLESSED VIRGIN

While St. Gertrude was once bemoaning her lack of service and devotion to our blessed Lord, she felt moved by the Holy Ghost to offer her the Heart of Jesus; which, she adds, our Lady received with exceeding joy, finding therein a delight greater far than all our service and devotion, so that no prayer, however fervent and recollected, could so gladden her maternal heart. St. Mechtilde also received a similar revelation.

I PRAISE and greet thee, O Virgin surpassingly sweet, in that intimate union wherewith thou art united to God above all creatures.

And in amends for all the negligences I have committed in thy service, I offer thee, O tender Mother, the most glorious and adorable Heart of Jesus Christ, with all that true and faithful filial love he showed thee in such perfection on earth, and will for ever show thee in heaven. Amen.

PRAYER OF ST. EDMUND

Composed by him to be repeated every day. Having omitted it one day, he saw in a vision of the night the holy evangelist St. John, who looked at him with a severe countenance, and said: Why have you omitted my prayer? And then, raising the sceptre he held in his hands with a threatening gesture, he commanded him never more to omit it.

O UNDEFILED and ever-blessed, only and incomparable Virgin Mary, Mother of God, Sanctuary of the Holy Ghost, Gate of the kingdom of heaven, through whom under God all the whole earth liveth; bow down thy compassionate ears to my unworthy supplications, O my Mother, and be to me, a miserable sinner, needful help and succour in all things. O most blessed John, thou beloved friend of Jesus, who wast chosen in thy purity by our Lord, and because of thy purity more tenderly beloved, and more deeply imbued with high and heavenly mysteries than thy brethren; O thou most glorious apostle and

evangelist, I invoke thee together with Mary
the Mother of the same our Lord Jesus Christ,
and beseech thee that thou wouldst, in union
with her, bestow upon me thine aid. O ye two
gems of heavenly brilliance, ye two lights
shining with divine lustre in the presence of
God, scatter with your bright beams the mists
and clouds of my sins. For you are they unto
whom, by reason of your spotless purity, our
Lord confirmed his love of predilection when
hanging on the cross, saying to the one: *Woman, behold thy son;* and to the other: *Behold
thy Mother.* Wherefore, in the sweetness of
that most holy love wherein you are joined
by our Lord himself as mother and as son,
I, a miserable sinner, now commend to both
my body and my soul, beseeching you to deign
to be my sure protectors, both inwardly and
outwardly, at every moment of my life, and
my compassionate intercessors with God. Demand for me, I beseech you, the salvation of
my soul and of my body, Grant, I implore
you, oh, grant that through your glorious
prayer the good and gentle Spirit, bounteous
Giver of all grace, may cleanse me from all
the defilements of my sins, may enlighten and
adorn me with all holy virtues, and enable me
to stand steadfast and to persevere unto the
end in the love of God and of my neighbours,
and when I have finished my course, may the
most gracious Paraclete lead me up to the
joys of his chosen. Who with the Father and
the Son, &c.

ASPIRATIONS OF A SINNER TO MARY

REMEMBER, O most compassionate Mother, that from the beginning it has never been heard that any who have fled unto thee for protection, or implored thy intercession, have been forsaken by thee. For to this end hath the Fountain of forgiveness been given to thee as thy Son, that thou mightest obtain grace for all who need, and that thine abundant charity might cover the multitude of our sins and our many defects. Wherefore, encouraged by this assurance, I have recourse to thee, and stand before thee in my misery and my defilement. Oh, despise me not for my innumerable and grievous sins, nor cast me away because of the exceeding loathsomeness and hardness of my heart. Thou knowest, O Mary, how deeply I am sunk in sins and vices, and how justly I have deserved all the most dreadful anger of thy Son. Cast me not away from thy favour, O most compassionate Mother, for thou art, after God, my surest confidence, and the chief, the only ground of my hope. For such is the trust I have in thee, that I shall never believe that I can perish, as long as I love thee and serve thee. O most holy Mother of God and of man, thou joy of all saints, thou solace of the wretched and refuge of the poor, I beseech thee, by that ineffable joy and sweetness thou didst feel when the incomprehensible Divinity took flesh of thee, and thus deigned to unite human nature to himself for ever in thy virginal womb, vouchsafe to undertake my cause, and to render me well-pleasing to the same thy well-beloved Son. Show him, O Mother, the breasts which he has sucked and the arms with which thou didst embrace him; set now before him all the toils and all the dolours thou didst suffer for his sake; show him that heart of thine, sweeter than the honeycomb, all glowing with the fire of his love; and so render him propitious unto me. O my most faithful advocate, turn on me, thy most unworthy servant, those pitying eyes of thine; and by the fragrance of that unimaginable delight thou didst feel as thou wentest up from this world to the royal court of heaven, leaning blissfully on thy Beloved, vouchsafe to be with me in the hour of my death; and in that dread hour offer for me to the most Holy Trinity the merits of that tranquil and consummate perfection which raised thee, on the day of thine Assumption, far above all human and angelic dignity, and made thee the object of his supreme and everlasting complacency. Amen.

INVITATION TO THE B.V.M. TO BE PRESENT AT OUR DEATH

O MOST holy Virgin Mary, in union with that most faithful love wherewith thy Son commended thee from his cross to the blessed John, I commend to thee my soul and my body, my thoughts, my words and my actions, my life and my death, and more especially that one last moment of my life on which eternity hangs. And as thou didst invite thy Son to thine own blessed departure, so I invite thee now to mine; beseeching thee, by that love wherewith thou didst stand beneath the cross on which thy Son was dying, and by the bitter tears thou didst shed when thou sawest him bow in death his sacred Head, that thou be not absent from me then, but be there to succour me with a mother's tenderness; for without thee I cannot die in peace. Refuse not, O most tender Mother, this my request, which I make to thee with all the earnestness and devotion of my heart; for if I die without thee, I most justly fear lest I perish everlastingly. For how shall I, fearful and frail as I am, stand then amidst the manifold and most grievous assaults of my enemies, unless thou be near to succour me? How shall I appear in the dread day of judgment, unless thou be my companion and my advocate? How give an account of my innumerable, my enormous, my most exceeding sins, unless thou plead my cause with thy Son, and obtain for me forgiveness of them all? Incline now thine ear to my supplication, O my blessed Mother; and by the love of thy Son come unto me in my last moments, that by thy availing succour I may be rescued from that appalling peril, and with thee attain to everlasting gladness. Amen.

THREE AVE MARIA FOR A GOOD DEATH

St. Mechtilde, having on one occasion asked the Blessed Virgin to assist her in the hour of her death, received this answer: You may feel assured of my presence and aid if you daily address to me this three-fold salutation.

HAIL, Mary, full of grace, the Lord is with thee; blessed art thou among women, and blessed is the fruit of thy womb, Jesus. Holy Mary, Mother of God, as God the Father in the grandeur of his omnipotence hath exalted thee and given thee power above all creatures, be with me, I beseech thee, in the hour of my death, and drive far from me all the snares and craft of my enemies. Amen.

Hail, Mary, &c. Holy Mary, Mother of God, as God the Son in the excellence of his unsearchable wisdom hath endued thee with so great knowledge, and filled thee with so great light that thou knowest the most Holy Trinity more truly and intimately than all saints, do thou so enlighten my soul in the hour of my death with the knowledge of the faith, that no error or ignorance may lead it astray. Amen.

Hail, Mary, &c. Holy Mary, Mother of God, as the Holy Spirit hath poured into thee the sweetness of his love with such abundance, that thou art after God the sweetest and most benign of beings, do thou pour into my soul at the hour of my death the sweetness of divine love, that its every bitterness may be rendered sweet to me. Amen.

Our Lord himself taught St. Gertrude to invoke his blessed Mother daily with the words: O thou our advocate, turn on us those pitying eyes of thine; *assuring her that she would thus receive great consolation in her last hour.*

THE SWORDS OF SORROW

Which pierced the heart of the Blessed Virgin in the Passion of her Son.

THE FIRST SWORD

O MOST sorrowful Virgin Mary, I recall to thy mind now that sharp sword of sorrow which pierced thy soul, when thy Beloved, thine only one, came to bid thee farewell, and to ask thy maternal blessing, ere he went forth to death. Remember, O Mother most afflicted, how thy heart was wrung when thy most tender and only Son, thy delight, so lovingly embraced thee for the last time, and with plaintive voice and tearful eyes bade thee farewell. Remember now your sighs and tears, when the hearts so joined together by the strongest ties of love were thus torn asunder, and pierced through with that keenest wound of sorrow. By that mournful going away of thy Son, and by all the bitter tears thou didst shed, I beseech thee, O Mary, be with me at the last when all my friends turn away from my lifeless body, and protect me with thy maternal blessing from all the snares of the enemy. Amen.

THE SECOND SWORD

O MOST afflicted Virgin Mary, I recall to thy mind now that keen sword of sorrow which pierced thy soul, when the blessed John came to tell thee that thy Son had been betrayed by Judas, seized by the Jews, dragged before Annas and Caiaphas, and there blasphemed and mocked, spit upon, buffeted, and overwhelmed with contumely and rude reproach. Remember, O thou most afflicted one, how these mournful tidings pierced thy heart. Oh, remember now the moans and wailing plaints with which thou didst fill the house, and how thou didst cry: O Jesus, my Son Jesus, who will grant me that I might die for thee, O Jesus, my Son, my Son! By that keenest sword of sorrow I beseech thee, O Mary, in my last hour, when my heart shall quake with anguish and the dread of death, do thou deign to cheer me with thy most holy presence, lest I sink in the abyss of despair. Amen.

THE THIRD SWORD

O MOST sad Virgin Mary, I recall to thy mind now that sword of sorrow which pierced thy heart, when thou didst behold thy Son led forth by Pilate, his sacred Body torn and bleeding, his Head crowned with thorns, defiled with spittings, so that there was no beauty in him, nor comeliness. Remember, O Mother most sad, how thy heart was torn when thou didst hear the Jews exclaim: Away with him, away with him! crucify him! Remember that keenest wound which was dealt upon thy heart when thou didst hear the sentence of an accursed death pronounced by Pilate. Remember all the compassion and the grief which wrung thy Mother's heart when thou didst see thy Son laden with his heavy cross, and led forth with direst ignominy to the hill of Calvary. Oh, who shall count thy sighs and tears, who shall tell the sorrows of thy most afflicted heart! I compassionate thee, O Mother most desolate, and I humbly beseech thee be with me in the dread hour of judgment, when I am overwhelmed with the accusations of the devil; and drive far from me then all mine enemies. Amen.

THE FOURTH SWORD

O MOST desolate Virgin Mary, I recall to thy mind now that sword of sorrow which pierced through thy heart, when thou didst behold thy Son raised high upon his cross, and fastened thereunto with three nails. O most sorrowful Mother, how was it that thy soul was not utterly crushed down and wrenched from thy body? How could it be that thine eyes did not fail for tears? Oh, remember now the sadness which filled thy heart when thou didst behold him blasphemed, mocked with vinegar and gall in his thirst, reputed viler and treated more ruthlessly than the very robbers. Remember thine ineffable anguish when thou didst see him fail and sink beneath his impetuous love and grief, his lips grow pale, his limbs quiver, his eyes grow glazed and dim; until at length his heart broke with a mighty pang, and with a loud cry he gave up the ghost. By these thy surpassing sorrows, O Mother most desolate, and by all thy groanings and tears, I beseech thee, be with me with the same love when I draw my last breath, when my heart shall break in the agony of death; and deign to receive my soul into thy hands as it goes forth from the body.

THE FIFTH SWORD

O VIRGIN Mary, Mother of dolours, I recall to thy mind now that sword of sorrow which pierced thy heart, when thou didst receive into thy bosom thy Son, taken down from the cross, and didst bedew his sacred Body with thy tears. Oh, what didst thou feel as thou didst gaze upon that Head pierced all around with thorns, that Side riven with the lance, those Hands and Feet dug through with the cruel nails, that beauteous Face marred with blows and defiled with spittings, and all that sacred Body torn with wounds, livid with stripes, and besmeared with blood. O most sorrowful Mother, how didst thou kiss that divine Face, and wash it with thy tears, and bewail the dishonour of thy Beloved. O Mother most forlorn, I pray thee, by all the sighs and groans wrung from thy heart, by all the sorrows and the wounds of thy soul, comfort mine in the hour when it goes forth from the body, wash it with thy tears, and receive it into thy maternal arms as thou didst receive the lifeless Body of thy Son, and lead it up to the joys of heaven. Amen.

A LITANY OF HOLY MARY

LORD have mercy.
Christ have mercy.
Lord have mercy.
Christ hear us.
Christ graciously hear us.
O God the Father, of heaven,
Have mercy on us.
O God the Son, Redeemer of the world,
Have mercy on us.
O God the Holy Ghost,
Have mercy on us.
Holy Trinity, one God,
Have mercy on us.

Holy Mary,
Holy Mother of God,
Holy Virgin of virgins,
Daughter of the Eternal Father,
Mother of the Son of God,
Spouse of the Holy Ghost,
Virgin most glorious,
Virgin most amiable,
Virgin most meek,
Virgin most gentle,

Pray for us.

Virgin most sweet,
Virgin most compassionate,
Virgin most gracious,
Virgin most faithful,
Virgin sweeter than the dropping honey-comb,
Delight of the Holy Trinity,
Temple of the living God,
Shrine of the Holy Ghost,
Glory of the heavenly Jerusalem,
Never-failing Spring of graces,
Stream of everlasting life,
Garden of heavenly delights,
Refuge of the sorrowful in spirit,
By thy sweetest name,
By the pity of thy Mother's heart,
By the love with which thou didst conceive Jesus, and bear him in thy most pure womb,
By the love with which thou didst bring forth Jesus, and lay him in the lowly manger,
By the love with which thou didst give him to suck of thy breasts,
By the love with which thou didst share with Jesus his joys and his sorrows,
By the love with which thou didst shed so many tears in his Passion,
By the love with which thou didst stand by the cross of Jesus,
By the love with which thou didst look upon Jesus risen,

Pray for us.

By the love with which thou didst gaze
 upon him ascending,
By the love with which thou didst receive
 the Holy Ghost,
By the love with which thou didst give thy
 spirit into his hands,
By the love with which thou wast taken up
 into heaven,
By the love with which thou wast welcomed
 into heaven, and exalted high above all
 creatures,
By the mutual love which unites thee to
 God,
By the love with which thou dost pity all
 sinners,
Holy Mary,
Intercede for us.

Lamb of God, who takest away the sins of the
 world,
Spare us, O Lord.

Lamb of God, who takest away the sins of the
 world,
Graciously hear us, O Lord.

Lamb of God, who takest away the sins of the
 world,
Have mercy on us.

Christ, hear us.
Christ, graciously hear us.

Ant. Through thee may we have access to
thy Son, O thou blessed one who hast found
grace, thou Mother of the Life and Mother of
Salvation; that by thee we may receive him

Pray for us.

who hath been given to us by thee. O our Lady, our advocate, may thy undefiled purity plead with him in excuse of our corruption; may thy humility, so pleasing to God, obtain from him forgiveness of our vanity; may thine abounding charity cover the multitude of our sins, and thy glorious fruitfulness render us fruitful in merits. Amen.

V. Pray for us, O holy Mother of God.

R. That we may be made worthy of the promises of Christ.

Let us pray

O LORD Jesus Christ, Son of the living God, who hast deigned to elect the blessed Mary ever Virgin above all creatures to be thy Mother, and in thy most lavish love hast watered and fertilised and blessed her with such abundant streams of manifold graces; we most humbly entreat thy clemency, by that mighty love wherewith thy Sacred Heart glowed towards her, that thou wouldst vouchsafe to be merciful to our sins, and to make us well-pleasing in thy sight, for the sake of the merits of the same thy most glorious Mother: who livest and reignest, &c.

PART VII

TO CERTAIN SAINTS

INSTRUCTION ON THE MANNER IN WHICH THE SAINTS ARE TO BE HONOURED

When St. Gertrude wished to honour any particular saint, she was accustomed to give God thanks for all the graces he had bestowed on that saint, by repeating several times the psalm: Laudate Dominum, omnes gentes. *She found by experience that when we thus thank God on behalf of any saint, he increases grace in our souls through the merit of that saint. On one occasion she seemed to see many persons clothed and adorned with the merits of St. Bernard, and was much astonished, as those persons had not done works like his.* What, then, *said St. Bernard to her,* is she less beautiful who is adorned with the ornaments of another, than she who is adorned with her own? Assuredly not; and thus it is in regard of the merits of the saints, obtained by those who praise God on their behalf; they are conferred on them with so great love that they will be to them matter of everlasting joy. *Remember this, therefore, and if you say the Divine Office, bow your head at the* Gloria Patri, *with the intention of thanking God for the graces he has bestowed on the saint whose feast you are celebrating.*

*On another occasion St. Gertrude offered to
the blessed Virgin* 150 Ave Maria's, *which she
had said in her honour; and it seemed to her
as though every word thus presented were a
piece of golden coin. And she felt within herself that whenever we commit the end of our
life to any saint by special prayers, those
prayers are borne up before the throne of the
Judge; and the saint to whom they were addressed is appointed by God the advocate of
those who have offered them, to provide them
all manner of good according to their need.*

*In like manner St. Mechtilde, having asked
one of her sisters departed, who had appeared
to her in radiant glory after her death:* Tell
me, my beloved Sister, of what avail to you
are the prayers we offer for you? *received this
answer:* I receive every word of them from
your mouth as so many blooming roses, which
I offer with joy to my Beloved. *And having
spoken thus, she showed her under her glorious mantle roses of exquisite bloom, having a
leaf of gold in the midst. And being asked
what was signified by that golden leaf, she answered:* It signifies those prayers which are offered of devotion, without obligation. *And
she added, moreover:* Whenever any one ad-
dresses his prayer to any saint, that saint receives all the words of his mouth as though
they were fresh blooming roses of spring. *And
if you say an* Our Father *to all saints, with
the intention, were it possible, of saying one*

for each of the saints, your intention is accepted by them as though you had really done so.

It is likewise most pleasing to the saints to salute them in and through the Sacred Heart of Jesus, and especially if you offer them that Divine Heart; because through it and from it they receive the most consummate and ecstatic delights.

TO ST. MICHAEL ARCHANGEL

HAIL, most glorious prince, Michael the Archangel! Hail, most noble leader of the heavenly host! Hail, honour and glory of the hierarchies of heaven! O most august prince, under what obligation dost thou lie to thy Creator, who, without any merit of thine own, hath endowed thee with such excellent might and adorned thee with such peerless virtues? O thou renowned warrior, thou ornament of Paradise, thou lustrous gem of the court of heaven, thou are the seal of likeness to God, full of wisdom and consummate in beauty. Every precious stone is thine adornment, and all the working of thy finished comeliness is of gold, in the delights of the Paradise of our God. Thou hast been appointed prince and captain to receive the souls of the elect, and to lead them into the Paradise of rejoicing. I recall to thy mind now, O most blessed prince, these and all other graces wherewith the boundless liberality of God hath enriched thee above all orders of angels; beseeching thee, by that mutual love which binds thy heart to the Divine Heart of Jesus, that thou wouldst deign to receive my soul at the moment of my departure, and to render the Judge propitious to me through thy intercession. Amen.

TO OUR GUARDIAN ANGEL

O MOST holy angel of God, appointed by him to be my guardian, I give thee thanks for all the benefits which thou hast ever bestowed on me in body and in soul. I praise and glorify thee that thou dost condescend to assist me, all miserable and worthless as I am, with such patient fidelity, and to defend me against all the assaults of my enemies. Blessed be the hour in which thou wast assigned me for my guardian, my defender, and my patron. Blessed be all thy love to me, and all thy care for me, wherewith thou dost unwearyingly further my salvation. In acknowledgment and return of all thy loving ministries to me from my youth up I offer thee the infinitely precious and noble Heart of Jesus, full and overflowing with all blessedness: beseeching thee to forgive me for having so often striven against thy holy inspirations, and saddened thee my nearest, dearest friend; and firmly purposing to obey thee henceforward, and most faithfully to serve my God. Amen.

TO ST. JOHN EVANGELIST

St. John was the special patron of St. Gertrude. Our Lord had assigned her to him, instructing her to say every day a Pater noster *in his honour, with the following prayer:*

O BLESSED John the Evangelist, I recall to thy mind now that most sweet and most affectionate fidelity thou didst feel in thy heart when our Lord taught thee, together with the other Apostles, this his own availing prayer: beseeching thee to obtain for me the grace to cleave faithfully to him, and to persevere to the end of my life. Amen.

Our Father, &c.

TO ST. BENEDICT

St. Benedict said to St. Gertrude: Whoever shall delight in recalling to my mind the grace which was vouchsafed me, of dying while I was standing and praying, I will assuredly be with him in the hour of his death, and will stand between him and his enemies, wherever their assault is most deadly and furious.

O MOST glorious patriarch, holy father Benedict, I recall to thy mind now that great and glorious grace bestowed on thee by our Lord, of breathing out thy last breath as thou stoodest praying, on which account thy lips now exhale a fragrance which ravishes all the saints with delight; beseeching thee to be with me in the hour of my death with loving fidelity, and to place thyself between me and the enemies round about me, wheresoever thou seest them rage most furiously against me; so that, protected by thy presence, I may escape all their snares, and reach the joys of heaven safe and blessed for ever. Amen.

TO ST. ANNE

Pope Alexander VI. granted an indulgence of twenty years to all who should devoutly repeat this prayer three times before an image of St. Anne.

HAIL, thou full of grace, the Lord is with thee; let thy grace be with me! Blessed art thou amongst women, and blessed be thy mother Anne, who brought thee forth, O Virgin Mary all immaculate; and of thee was born Jesus Christ, the Son of the living God. Amen.

TO ST. MARY MAGDALEN

St. Mary Magdalen said to St. Mechtilde: Whosoever shall give God thanks for all the tears I shed upon the feet of Jesus, &c., our most merciful God will grant him through my intercession remission of all his sins before his death, and a great increase of love to God.

O MOST merciful Jesus, I give thee thanks for that work of piety which the blessed Mary Magdalen wrought on thee when she washed thy feet with her tears, and wiped them with the hair of her head, and kissed them and anointed them with fragrant ointment; whereby she obtained from thee such signal grace that thou didst pour into her heart and soul so great love of thee that she could love nothing apart from thee: beseeching thee that by her merits and intercessions thou wouldest vouchsafe to me tears of true repentance, and pour into my heart thy divine love.   Amen.

PRAYER TO JESUS

Through the merits of St. Gertrude

Our Lord promised St. Gertrude that if any one should praise God for her, and give him thanks for the love wherewith he had chosen her from eternity, &c., he would assuredly grant him whatever he asked, provided that it tended to his salvation.

O MOST compassionate Jesus, Giver of all good and all grace, may all that are in the round world and the depth of the sea and the compass of heaven give thanks to thee and praise thee with that infinite, everlasting, and unchanging praise which floweth forth from thee and floweth back unceasingly upon thee again, for the exceeding love wherewith thou didst shed into the heart and soul of thy beloved spouse Gertrude so great a flood of graces and of loving-kindnesses, and didst reveal to the world the mysteries of thy tender compassion through her, thine own chosen and peculiar instrument. Wherefore from my inmost heart I render thee utmost thanks; and I beseech thee, on behalf of all in heaven, on earth, or in purgatory; through that ineffable divine love wherewith thou didst from all eternity elect to special grace thy loving and most faithful servant, and didst in thine own appointed time draw her so sweetly to thee, and unite her so intimately to thyself, and dwell with such delight in her heart, and crown her life with an end so blessed; that thou wouldst condescend graciously to hear and to answer my petition. I recall to thy mind now, O most compassionate Jesus, the promise thou madest to thy beloved spouse in thy great and superabounding goodness, that thou wouldst most assuredly grant the prayers to all who come to thee through her merits and intercession, in all matters concerning their salvation; binding thyself, moreover, if thou didst not at once grant their petition, to bestow on them three-fold in thine own good time, from the omnipotence, the wisdom, and the tender kindness of the adorable Trinity. Calling thus to thy mind this thy faithful promise, I beseech thee, leave me not desolate, but bestow on me the salutary effect of my petition. Amen.

AN EFFICACIOUS PRAYER TO ST. GERTRUDE

I PRAISE and greet thee, O most blessed Virgin Gertrude, through the sweetest Heart of Jesus thy Spouse; and through that Heart I magnify the goodness and condescension of the ever-adorable Trinity for all the grace which has ever flowed forth from that unfathomable abyss for thy salvation; beseeching thee, by that mutual love which united thy pure heart to the Sacred Heart of Jesus, that thou wouldst look on me as commended to thy care in life and in death, and be my faithful advocate with God. Amen.

PRAYER TO ST. GERTRUDE IN TIME OF TEMPTATION

One who was grievously tempted with evil thought and almost brought to consent to them, took by a holy inspiration a relic of St. Gertrude and applied it to her heart, saying with great confidence:

O LORD Jesus, I beseech thee by that love wherewith thou didst choose the heart of thy elect one, freed from every earthly affection, to be thine own exclusive abode, and didst fill it with spiritual gifts; vouchsafe to deliver me from this fierce temptation through her merits and intercession. Amen.

And as soon as she had thus prayed, the temptation left her. Imitate her example; and if you have not a relic of the saint, apply her image to your heart.
St. Francis directed a brother who was suffering temptation to say with devotion: Glory be

to the Father, and to the Son, and to the Holy
Ghost. *And when he had done so, the temptation vanished. And this has been often done
with much fruit.*

THANKSGIVING FOR THE GRACES BESTOWED ON
ST. MECHTILDE

*Our Lord said to a devout person: I will gra-
ciously incline myself towards those who love
my beloved Mechtilde for my sake, and will
draw them to me. And those who shall give
me thanks for having exalted her so highly, I
will make them partakers of her merits, and
grant them divine consolation in the hour of
death.*

I GIVE thanks to thy goodness, O my God;
I give thanks to thy condescension, that
thou hast chosen thy beloved and blessed
Mechtilde to so great grace, and hast adorned
her with such immense gifts and virtues. I rejoice together with thee, O compassionate
Jesus, and I give thee thanks for all the good
thou hast wrought in her, and wilt work in her
for evermore. I thank thee for that abounding
joy and that tranquil peace thou didst find in
her. I give thee thanks for that ravishing influx of grace wherewith thou didst incline
thine heart towards her, and for all the holy
operation of thy Spirit within her. And, lastly,
I thank thee for that perfect and untroubled
delight thou didst take in her; beseeching thee

devoutly to make me a partaker of her merits, and to adorn me with the splendour of her virtues. Amen.

PRAYER TO A MARTYR

I SALUTE thee and venerate thee, O most holy martyr of Christ, St. N., I bless and magnify the infinite goodness and condescension of the ever-adorable Trinity for all the graces which he hath deigned to bestow on thee of his exceeding and most bounteous love. I bless the boundless liberality of the divine compassion which so gently prevented thee with the blessings of sweetness, and hath gloriously adorned thy head with the triumphant crown of martyrdom in the heavens. O holy N., most blessed martyr of Christ, invincible soldier in that army whose garments are sprinkled with blood; thou art a foundation-stone of the faith, and a column of strength. Thou art a glorious hero of the Church, the honour and the glory of Paradise; blessed art thou amongst martyrs, and beautiful in thy form above the inhabitants of heaven. For the increase of thy glory and blessedness I offer thee the most worshipful Heart of Jesus Christ, so consummate and perfect in all good things through its union with his Divinity; devoutly beseeching thee, by all and every drop of thy precious blood which thou hast shed, by all the cruel wounds thou didst receive, and by the bitter anguish thou didst endure in

heart and soul and body, that thou wouldst be
with me in the hour of my death, which I
commend to thee with sure trust; and wouldst
offer to Jesus my Judge, in compensation for
the merits which I lack, the virtues whereby
thou knowest thyself to be more especially
pleasing in his sight. Amen.

PRAYER TO A CONFESSOR

HAIL, holy N., illustrious confessor of
Christ, glory and adornment of his holy
Church. Thou art the sweet budding rose of
charity, the lily of purity, the beaming star of
sanctity. Like the morning star in the midst
of a cloud, and as the moon at the full, so
didst thou shine forth in the splendour of thy
virtues. O most blessed N., what thanks dost
thou owe to God for all his gifts to thee, in
that he chose thee from eternity in his unsearchable wisdom, justified thee freely, and
made thee honourable and worthy of his
grace; in that he hath delivered thee from all
evil and misery in his strong and prevailing
love, and hath made all the events of thy life,
the evil as well as the good, work together
unto thy good and thy salvation. Wherefore
I give thanks to thy most loving Creator, and
I magnify and extol with thee the omnipotence,
the wisdom, and the goodness of the transcendently glorious Trinity, which has deigned
to decree and give effect to thy predestination
unto so great holiness, and to adorn thee to-

gether with himself with a crown of justice in the kingdom of his glory. O blessed N., most holy friend of Jesus, remember me, a miserable sinner, who invoke thee with all the devotion of my heart. I commend to thee my life and my death, and especially my last parting breath; beseeching thee, by that love wherewith thou didst cleave so fast to God and serve him so devoutly, that thou wouldst deign to offer to God in satisfaction for my sins all the mortifications, the austerities, and the penance which thou didst so willingly undertake and so lovingly accomplish for the glory of his Name. Amen.

PRAYER TO A VIRGIN AND MARTYR

HAIL, holy N., glorious virgin and martyr. Hail, sweetest spouse of Jesus, thou vessel of election of the Holy Ghost; like as the rose amongst thorns, and as a star in the midst of a cloud, so didst thou shine forth upon the darkness of the world. I salute and bless thee a thousandfold in that union wherewith thy loving soul is one spirit with God, and I rejoice and exult in the victory which thou hast gained in thy glorious strife. I congratulate thee on the twofold crown, of virginity and of martyrdom, wherein thou shinest gloriously forth as a star in the firmament. For the increase of thy joy, thy glory, and thy blessedness, I offer thee the sweetest Heart of my Jesus, together with all his filial love to God the Father in his

Divinity, and to Mary his Mother in his Humanity, and through that sacred Heart I commend myself to thy especial care and patronage, that by thy most holy sufferings and death, and by the merits of thy pure and virgin blood, I may obtain forgiveness of my sins, and the sure protection of divine grace in life and in death. Amen.

PRAYER TO A VIRGIN

HAIL, holy N., graceful virgin, unspotted spouse of Jesus, thou art full of grace and of love, lustrous with honour, resplendent with charity. O blessed N., I recall to thy mind now that ineffable grace which our Lord bestowed upon thee, when he set thee apart even from thy mother's womb, and chose thee into the number of his especially beloved ones. Blessed be the perfection of thy snow-white purity, and the gentle charm of thy most chaste love; for with one hair of thy neck and with one of thine eyes thou hast wounded the heart of thy Lord the King. Thou art a lily of virginity glistening in thy whiteness, an unfading flower of purity, who drawest all saints after the sweet odour of thy perfumes, and dost gladden and refresh them with the marvellous radiance of thy light. Thou art a spotless lamb, clothed upon with the snowy fleece of chastity, and thou followest the Lamb whithersoever he goeth, and with most ravishing melody dost sing thy virgin hymn. I beseech thee, O blessed N., by that love wherewith Christ doth bestow on thee the rewards of everlasting bliss, blot out all the stains of my manifold corruptions, and with thy undefiled virginity cover the foulness of my defilement, and obtain for me, through the favour thou hast found with God, that I may never henceforward, by thought or word or deed, sin against the sacredness of purity. Amen.

PRAYER TO A SAINT ON HIS FEAST-DAY

O HOLY N., I praise thee, bless thee, and glorify thee, and congratulate thee with all my heart on all the glory and honour which are rendered to thee to-day, through the boundless liberality of the divine goodness. I recall to thy mind now the overflowing gladness with which thou didst rejoice when thou wast presented before the face of the glory of God by the ministry of holy angels, to receive from him thine everlasting reward. Remember, O most blessed saint, all thy honour and thy glad rejoicing when the hand of God placed the crown of the kingdom on thy head, and thy soul was set upon the throne of its glory. For these and all other benefits and graces which have ever been bestowed upon thee by the God of majesty, I adore, praise, and bless his unutterable goodness, that he hath poured out upon thee in such abundance the flood of his sweetest compassion; and as the bond of that perpetual love and faithfulness in which I desire to bind myself to thee, I offer thee the sweetest Heart of my Jesus, that treasure of all good things, together with all the love and the condescension he hath ever showed thee upon earth, and now showeth thee in the heavens. And, finally, with most assured trust I commend myself to thy most holy prayers; beseeching and imploring thee that in the dread hour of my death thou wouldst offer unto the Lord, in satisfaction for my manifold negligences, all that collected fervour with which thou didst stand before God perfect and complete on this the day of thine entrance into Paradise.   Amen.

Invocation of all saints, which our Lord taught to St. Mechtilde, and commanded her to recite.

O YE holy Patriarchs and Prophets, I salute you in the sweetest Heart of Jesus; beseeching you to deign to offer unto God for me the ardent yearning desire you felt for the Incarnation of Jesus.

O ye holy Apostles, I salute you in the sweetest Heart of Jesus; beseeching you to deign to offer unto God for me that faithfulness and constancy wherewith you continued with Jesus in his temptations, and gathered unto him a faithful people by your preaching.

O ye holy Martyrs, I salute you in the sweetest Heart of Jesus; beseeching you to deign to offer unto God for me that patience with which you shed your blood for his love.

O ye holy Confessors, I salute you in the sweetest Heart of Jesus; beseeching you to deign to offer unto God for me that sanctity which shone forth in your words and your example.

O ye holy Virgins, I salute you in the sweetest Heart of your divine Spouse; beseeching you to deign to offer unto God for me that purity and chastity whereby you have merited to stand now so near to Jesus in heaven.

O all ye Saints of God, I salute and venerate you all in the sweetest Heart of Jesus your Lord, and through it I render thanks to God for all the good which has ever flowed forth from it for your salvation; beseeching you all in general, and each one of you in particular, to deign to offer unto God for me, a miserable sinner, all those virtues and perfections which render you most especially well-pleasing to God. Amen.

LITANY OF ALL SAINTS

LORD have mercy.
Christ have mercy.
Lord have mercy.
Christ hear us.
Christ graciously hear us.
O God the Father, of heaven,
Have mercy on us.
O God the Son, Redeemer of the world,
Have mercy on us.

O God the Holy Ghost,
Have mercy on us.
Holy Trinity, one God,
Have mercy on us.
Holy Mary,
All ye holy Angels and Archangels,
All ye holy Thrones and Dominations,
All ye holy Princedoms and Powers,
All ye holy Virtues of the heavens,
All ye holy Cherubim and Seraphim,
All ye holy Patriarchs and Prophets,
All ye holy Apostles and Evangelists,
All ye holy Martyrs and Confessors,
All ye holy Bishops and Doctors,
All ye holy Priests and Levites,
All ye holy Monks and Hermits,
All ye holy Penitents and Pilgrims,
All ye holy Virgins and Widows,
All ye who have served God in holy matrimony,
All ye holy Innocents,
All ye Saints of God,
  Intercede for us.

Pray for us.

Jesus, Crown of all thy saints,
By their virtues and merits,
By their patience and humility,
By their penance and mortification,
By their fasts and watchings,
By their weariness and toils,
By their poverty and want,
By their pilgrimages and prayers,

Have mercy on us.

By their devotion and their love,
By their sighs and their longings,
By their charity and alms,
By their compassion and mercy,
By their persecutions and martyrdom,
By their bonds and imprisonment,
By their pains and torments,
By their wounds and stripes,
By their cruel death,
By the shedding of their blood,
By all the adversities and the miseries which they endured for thy glory,
By the love wherewith thou hast loved them from eternity,
By the love wherewith thou didst draw them to thyself,
By the love wherewith thou didst dwell in their hearts,
By the love wherein thou didst confer on them such manifold graces,
By the love wherewith thou didst receive them into heaven,
By the love wherewith thou art ever bestowing on them their everlasting reward,
By the mutual love which unites them to thee, Jesus Christ,

Have mercy on us.

Lamb of God, who takest away the sins of the world,

Spare us, O Lord.

Lamb of God, who takest away the sins of the world,

Graciously hear us, O Lord.

Lamb of God, who takest away the sins of the
  world,
Have mercy on us.
Jesus, hear us.
Jesus, graciously hear us.
  V. Pray for us, all ye saints of God.
  R. That by your merits we may attain to
everlasting life.

Let us pray

O LORD Jesus Christ, Crown of thy saints,
  do thou have mercy on thy people, who
are called by thy Name, and by the merits of
all thy saints be merciful to our iniquities.
Remember all the faithfulness and the love
which they kept always to thee even unto
death. Behold, their innocent blood so ruthlessly shed crieth unto thee from the ground,
imploring thy mercy. Be thou appeased O our
Lord, by their merits which we now offer thee,
and grant us to enjoy their society in heaven,
on whose merits and patronage we rely on
earth. Who livest, &c. Amen.

PART VIII

PRAYERS FOR DIFFERENT NECESSITIES

KISSING THE FIVE WOUNDS FOR THE WELFARE OF THE CHURCH

When St. Gertrude, inspired by God, had kissed the Five Wounds of Jesus in the manner which follows, it was revealed to her that whenever any one does any good work, however small it be, for the glory of God, or says an Our Father *for the welfare of the Church, the Son of God receives that work with ineffable delight as the fruit of his Passion, gives thanks to God the Father for it, blesses it, and in blessing multiplies it, and distributes it to the whole Church to promote the everlasting salvation of his elect.*

AT THE WOUND OF THE LEFT FOOT

O SWEETEST Jesus, with all the loving affection of my heart I kiss the wound of thy left Foot, in expiation of all the sins which have been ever committed in thy whole Church by thought, or desire, or intention; beseeching thee that thou wouldst vouchsafe to impart to it for its cleansing that perfect and sufficing expiation whereby thou hast purged away the sins of the whole world. Amen.

AT THE WOUND OF THE RIGHT FOOT

O MOST compassionate Jesus, with all the loving affection of my heart I kiss the wound of thy right Foot, for all the omissions made by thy whole Church in good thoughts, in holy desires, and pious intentions; beseeching thee that thou wouldst now vouchsafe to impart to it for the supply of its omissions that most perfect and sufficing satisfaction by which thou didst pay all the debt of the whole race of man. Amen.

AT THE WOUND OF THE LEFT HAND

O MOST loving Jesus, with most devout intention of soul I kiss the wound of thy left Hand, in expiation of all the sins of word and of deed committed by the whole world; beseeching thee that thou wouldst vouchsafe to impart to thy Church for its cleansing that most perfect and sufficing satisfaction whereby thou hast made atonement for all our sins, of word and deed. Amen.

AT THE WOUND OF THE RIGHT HAND

O MOST kind Jesus, with most profound devotion I kiss the wound of thy right Hand, in satisfaction for all the negligences of thy whole Church in useful words and good works; beseeching thee that thou wouldst vouchsafe to impart to it for the supply of all its defects that consummate perfection wherewith thy Divinity caused thy Humanity to shine with such transcendent glory. Amen.

AT THE WOUND OF THE SIDE

O MOST gentle Jesus, with the deepest love of my heart I kiss the loving wound of thy most sacred Side; beseeching thee that after having bestowed on thy holy Bride the Church sufficing expiation of all its sins, and perfect satisfaction for all its negligences and omissions, thou wouldst, according to the multitude of thy divine compassions, impart to it for the increase of its everlasting bliss the merits of all thy most holy life and conversation, wherein thou dost now shine forth with such effulgence in the presence of God the Father. Amen.

OFFERING OF THE MERITS OF CHRIST FOR THE SINS OF ALL MANKIND

St. Gertrude was accustomed to say, under the guidance of the Holy Ghost, five Our Father's in honour of the Five Wounds of our Lord, and in satisfaction for all the sins of the five senses committed by the whole race of men. She added also three Our Father's in satisfaction for all the sins of the three principal faculties of the soul committed by all mankind, as well as in supply of all their omissions and defects.

OFFERING OF OUR LORD'S PRAYER

O SWEETEST Jesus, I offer thee this prayer in union with that most perfect intention wherewith thou didst sanctify it in thy sacred Heart, and give it forth to us for our salvation; in satisfaction for all our sins committed, and for all the negligences and the defects arising from human frailty, ignorance, or ill-will, against thy irresistible omnipotence, thy unsearchable wisdom, and thy superabounding gratuitous goodness. Amen.

When she had made this offering our gracious Lord, as though propitiated by the ineffable complacency with which he looked on her, stretched forth his Hand, and gave her his loving benediction, signing her with the sign of the cross from the crown of her head to her feet. Let us strive, by imitating the saint, to gain a like blessing.

On another occasion our Lord said to her: Recite thirty-three Our Father's, *and thus buy of me my holy conversation and life while for thirty-three years I was working salvation in the midst of the earth. And I communicate this fruit of my work to my whole Church for its salvation and my glory. And when she had done this she saw in her spirit the whole Church adorned as a bride with all the fruit of the most holy life and conversation of Christ. You may gather how pleasing it is to Christ to pray for his Church, from these following words which he said to St. Mechtilde: If any one, of pure love to God, prays for another person as though he were praying for himself, his prayer shall enlighten the heavenly Jerusalem like the morning sun.*

PRAYER FOR THE WHOLE CHURCH

St. Gertrude said to our Lord on one occasion: Behold, O Lord, I offer thee the desires and petitions of all who have commended themselves to my unworthy prayers. And the Lord said to her: Thou hast enkindled and inflamed my heart with as many torches of love as are the persons whom thou dost represent before me. Then said the saint: Lord, teach me how to come before thee for all the members of thy Church, and I will enkindle in thy Heart as many torches of love as there are persons in the whole universal Church. Our Lord answered her thus: You may do what you desire in these four ways: by praising me for having created them; by giving me thanks for the benefits I have bestowed on them, &c., as follows:

O MOST compassionate Jesus, I praise, bless and glorify thee with the love of my whole heart for the creation of all those whom thou hast deigned to form after thine own image and likeness, and I render thee thanks for all the benefits that thou hast ever bestowed, or shalt ever hereafter bestow, on them. In union with thy most exceeding anguish I pour out now my complaint before thee, with true sorrow and repentance for every manner in which they have ever hindered or frustrated thy grace; and I most devoutly pray for all men, that each in his appointed place may be made perfect in every good work, to thy everlasting praise and glory. Amen.

LAVDATE REPEATED THRICE FOR OUR OWN SINS OR THOSE OF OTHERS

St. Gertrude said to our Lord: Teach me, O most loving Master, with what prayer I may most sweetly soothe and propitiate thine anger, excited by the sins of men. Our Lord answered her thus: It will be very pleasing to me to recite the Our Father, *or the psalm:* Laudate Dominum, omnes gentes, *three times, and offer them to God in the following manner:*

Our Father, *or,* Laudate.

O MOST holy Father, in expiation of all the earthly and carnal delights and the perverse desires with which any human heart, and in particular my own, has ever been ensnared, I offer thee all the toil of the most sacred Heart of thine only-begotten Son, wherewith he was wearied upon earth for our salvation; all its praise, its giving of thanks, its plaints, its movements, its yearnings, and its love. Amen.

Our Father, *or*, Laudate.

O MOST holy Father, in expiation of all the sins committed in thy holy Church, and particularly my own, by gluttony and drunkenness, and by the multiplication of useless and hurtful words, I offer thee all the gracious words uttered by the most sacred Lips of thine only-begotten Son; all his abstinence and temperance, his silence, his unwearied preaching and his prayers, wherein he toiled for our salvation. Amen.

Our Father, *or*, Laudate.

O MOST holy Father, in expiation of all the sins which any member of thy Church, and in particular I myself, have ever committed in any manner, or by the misuse of any member of the body, I offer thee now every movement of the most sacred Body of thine only-begotten Son; the movements of all his most holy Limbs, all the whole course of his most perfect conversation and life, together with all the bitterness of the most sinless Passion and Death which he endured for the redemption of the human race. Amen.

A VERY EFFICACIOUS PRAYER FOR OUR RELATIONS AND FRIENDS

While St. Gertrude was thus praying for all who had an especial claim on her affection, the merciful Lord, recalling to mind in the light of his divine knowledge the necessities of each, vouchsafed to display towards them his tender and most loving compassion.

O MOST kind and gentle Jesus, I commend all those who have asked my unworthy prayers to thy divine knowledge and love, under the guidance of which thou didst come down to earth from the bosom of thy Father to save man. And in union with that love wherewith thou didst commend thy Spirit to thy Father, I commend them all to thy sacred Heart, and enclose them all therein; and I offer and set it forth before thee, in union with that love wherewith thou didst take it unto thyself, a true human heart, for the salvation of all the human race, and hast often given it as a token of thy special friendship to thy well-beloved friends; beseeching thee to take from its infinite treasures wherewithal to bless those for whom I pray, or am bound to pray. Amen.

Thus our Lord taught St. Gertrude to pray. Then add an Our Father, *and offer it thus:*

O GOOD Jesus, I offer thee this prayer to thine everlasting praise, and that through it thou mayest shed forth thy benefits and blessings on those who are dear to thee and to me, according to the good pleasure of thy divine compassion. Amen.

In like manner St. Gertrude was accustomed to offer, with the approval of our Lord, a Miserere *for all who were dear to her.*
That you may know how useful it is to pray for others, hear what our Lord said to St. Gertrude on one occasion: Even as it cannot be that a man's feet should be pierced through, and his heart not feel a thrill of anguish and compassion, so it is impossible that my fatherly pity should not look with an eye of mercy on him who, although he feels himself bowed down beneath the burden of his own transgressions, and needs first of all for himself the healing balm of divine forgiveness, still prays unceasingly for the salvation of his neighbour.

FOR OUR ENEMIES

When St. Gertrude had prayed the following prayer, it seemed to her as though our Lord fell down before the Face of God the Father, and offered for her the fruit of all his most holy life and conversation, in expiation of all her sins.

O LORD Jesus, in union with that love and that surpassing sweetness with which, amidst the unutterable anguish and sorrows of thy Passion, thou didst pray for those who crucified thee, saying: *Father, forgive them,* I beseech thee with all the love of my heart that thou wouldst now vouchsafe to forgive all who have ever or in any way offended against me. Amen.

PRAYER IN ANY TRIBULATION

When St. Gertrude and her sisters had long prayed to God in a certain affliction without receiving any answer, she said at length: How is it, O thou most tender Lover of my soul, that thou thus deferrest my hope? Then our Lord answered her, saying: It were not to be wondered at that a father should permit his son to ask him for a piece of money, if at each demand he laid up for him a hundred. In like manner do not wonder if I seem to defer to grant your petition in this matter; for as often as you pray to me in this matter, be it only by one word or by one thought, I lay up in store for you far more than a hundredfold of eternal good things.

O FATHER of mercies and God of all consolation, vouchsafe, I beseech thee, to look on me with the eyes of thy compassion, as thou didst look upon thy beloved Son when, in the Garden of Olives, he cried unto thee in the sore anguish of his spirit, and bedewed the ground with his sweat of blood. Is it not thy will, O most pitiful Father, that we should flee unto thee in all our necessities, and call upon thee to turn away from us all our perils? Seeing, therefore, that thou willest that we should pray to thee and call upon thy Name, I beseech thee in accordance with thy will that thou wouldst deliver me from this tribulation, in thy own most adorable good pleasure. O most tender Father, incline the ears of thy compassion to my prayers, all unworthy as they are, and draw me out of this great strait. Before the eyes of thy mercy, at the feet of thy tender love, I lay open all the anguish of my heart and the distress of my spirit, and I offer it to thee that thou mayest do with it as seemeth best in thy sight. O sweet Jesus, by all the anguish and the distress thou didst undergo for our salvation, let this chalice pass from me. O most compassionate Jesus, I offer thee that transcending prayer which thy sweat of blood in view of the agony of death rendered so fervent, and which the glowing love of thy Divinity rendered so effectual; beseeching thee now to hear me through its virtue, and to deliver me from this affliction. Wherefore I implore thee, with thine own intention and resignation, with the feelings of thine own heart and the words of thy sacred lips, saying: Abba, Father, all things are possible to thee; remove this chalice from me; nevertheless not what I will, but what thou wilt. Amen.

PRAYER OF ONE WHO IS SICK OR AFFLICTED

When on one occasion St. Mechtilde was ill, and had poured out her complaint before our Lord, he said to her: Lay all thy pains in my Heart, and I will grant thee all the alleviation I have ever granted to any of my saints. And like as my Passion brought forth ineffable fruit, so if you commend your sickness to me it shall bring forth increase of honour to the blessed, of merit to the just, and of forgiveness to sinners.

O MOST loving Jesus, I accept with most ready will this sickness [*or,* this affliction] which thou hast sent me from thy paternal Heart in token of thy love, and I offer it to thee with thankfulness, in that same love wherein thou hast sent it upon me. Wherefore I lay all my pain and my anguish in thy most sacred Heart, beseeching thee that thou wouldst deign to unite them to thine own most bitter Passion, to absorb them therein and render them perfect and acceptable to thee. And since by reason of the multitude of my sorrows and pains I cannot praise thee as I ought, do thou praise thy Father for my sufferings with that praise wherewith thou didst praise him upon the cross in thine own extremest agony. And as thou didst give him thanks with all thy heart for all the contumely and the pain which he laid upon thee, so do thou thank him for these my sufferings. And finally, with that same love wherewith thou didst accept all thy wounds and all thy reproaches and offer them to thy Father with perfect gratitude, do thou offer to him this my outward and inward affliction, together with thy most holy Passion, to his everlasting praise and glory. Amen.

OFFERING OF ANY PAIN OR GRIEF

Whenever any pain or grief comes upon you, offer it immediately to the divine love, as our Lord taught St. Mechtilde.

O MY sweet Love, I offer thee this little smart, and commend it to thee with that same intention wherewith thou hast brought it down to me from the Heart of Jesus, beseeching thee to record it for me on high together with my deepest thankfulness.

ACT OF RESIGNATION IN SICKNESS

A sick or dying person can do nothing better than to commit himself wholly and unreservedly to the divine will, and to profess his perfect readiness to accept from his hand all suffering, and even death itself. And whosoever does this with his whole heart may be sure that he shall enter heaven without passing through purgatory, even though he have committed innumerable sins. So we are taught by Tauler, Blosius, Suso, and others. Wherefore the sick person should often recite the following prayer, or have it recited for him.

BEHOLD, O almighty and most merciful God, thy unworthy servant offer and resign myself to thee wholly and unreservedly, for thine everlasting praise and glory, that thou mayest do in me, both in body and in soul, all thine adorable will; and I make this offering in union with that love wherewith thy Son offered himself to thee while hanging on the cross. And I profess from my heart my readiness to endure with patience, and for the sake of thy love and thy glory, all the pains and anguish of this my sickness, and even death itself, and all the evils and the chastisement which the severity of thy divine justice may lay upon me in time or in eternity. Wherefore, in thy presence and in presence of all thy saints, I declare and protest, that were it in my power to live a thousand years amidst all the pleasures and delights the heart of man can conceive or desire, I would nevertheless choose rather for thy love and thy glory to die at this time, if it be thy holy will. And with the fullest resignation of myself into thy hands, I say and repeat a thousand times with heart and mouth: Not my will, but thine be done, O most loving Jesus, in me, by me, in all that concerns me, in time and in eternity. Amen.

PRAYER FOR A SICK PERSON

When St. Gertrude was about to pray for a sick person, she asked our Lord what prayer would be most pleasing in his sight, and received this answer: Say the few following words for him with a devout heart; and as often as you repeat them, both you and the sick person shall receive a notable increase of merit. Those who are sick may say this prayer for themselves, making the needful changes.

O LORD Jesus, I beseech thee, by that love wherewith thou didst bear all our languors and carry all our sorrows, that thou wouldst sustain the patience of this thy servant who is sick, and overrule for thy greater glory and his most real advantage all these moments of his suffering in conformity with the decree which thy fatherly Heart hath decreed from eternity for his everlasting salvation. Amen.

THREE MOST EFFICACIOUS PRAYERS FOR A HAPPY DEATH

O BELOVED truth, O just equity of God, how shall I appear before thy face, bearing my iniquity, the guilt of the waste and loss of my life, and the burden of my exceeding negligence! I have not only spent in vain the talent of time entrusted to me; I have squandered it, wasted it, lost it all. And where shall I go, whither turn, whither flee from thy presence? O just equity of God, judging all things in number, weight, and measure, and weighing all things in thy most true and strict balance; woe, woe is me if I fall into thy hands, and have no advocate to plead my cause. O good Jesus, I flee unto thee, unto thee I sigh from my inmost heart; do thou answer for me, do thou obtain forgiveness for my sins; plead thou my cause, that my soul may live for thy sake. O Jesus, my Love, who for love of me wast seized and bound and dragged to an unrighteous tribunal, that on thee might be laid the sins of the whole world, though there was in thee no sin nor stain save that thou didst love me and bear my sins, I take thee this day for my Advocate and Friend at the bar of God. O my sweetest Jesus, beloved pledge of my redemption, do thou come with me to my judgment. Be thou thyself my Judge and my Advocate. Tell forth all that thou hast done for me, all thy thoughts of love towards me, at what a price thou hast made me thine. Thou hast lived for me, that I might not perish; thou hast borne my sins, that I might not be crushed by their weight; and thou hast died for me, that I might not die; and thou hast bestowed all thou hast on me, that in thy merits I might be rich. Wherefore judge me in the hour of my death according to that sinlessness which thou hast conferred upon me in thyself, in that thou hast paid all my debt, condescending to be judged and condemned for me. Amen.

SECOND PRAYER

O GENTLE goodness and amiable mercy of God, which alone dost restrain the anger of the Prince, and dost encompass and adorn the throne of the King with clemency; shelter me beneath thy wings, that I may be safe from the evils which threaten me, and which my many and great negligences make me fear. Behold, now the Creditor stands at the door, demanding from me account of the life entrusted to me. Now the Exactor claims from me the tribute of my time, and I dare not appear before him, for I have not wherewithal to pay. O Jesus, my Love, refuge of all in distress, appease thy Father towards me. Speak for me a word in charity; say, I will ransom him. O Jesus, my Love, who for me wast harshly bound to the pillar and cruelly scourged, who wast painfully crowned and scoffingly saluted; be thou my Advocate and my Patron. Judaea disowned thee for her King, that I might have thee all my own. Do thou quicken and refresh my soul now through thine own unutterable sorrows and griefs, and may that most bitter chastisement of our peace which the Father laid upon thee acquit all my debts. Anoint and soothe all my senses with the blood which flowed from thy most glorious Head, and efface all their stains through the anguish of thy most holy Body. May the most blameless use thou didst make of all thy senses cover all my faults and supply all my defects, that I may find all I want in thee, who hast delivered thyself all for me. Amen.

THIRD PRAYER

O SWEET compassion, O dear liberality of my God, that openest thy bosom to all, and art the refuge of all the poor; I shudder with dread at thought of my sins of commission, I blush and am ashamed at my sins of omission, I greatly fear by reason of the wretched waste I have made of my whole life. I quail with awe while I look onward to that scrutiny wherewith thou wilt search me when thou, my God, shalt enter in judgment with me. For if thou shalt require at my hands an account of the time and the talents which thou hast entrusted to me, I find within me no answer worthy of thine exceeding love to me. What shall I do, or whither betake myself? Oh, spare me and have mercy on me, Jesus, my Love, who for me wast condemned to an unjust death, laden with thy heavy cross, fastened to thy cross with cruel nails, mocked in thy thirst with vinegar and gall, till thou didst die for me a bitter death. Thou hast given thy soul for my soul, thy life for my life, thy death for my death. Thou didst once offer thyself upon the cross, and thou dost even now daily offer to God the Father upon the altar that Sacrifice which transcends all merit, and is infinitely more than enough to pay all my debt. Oh, by this Sacrament renew my life, and restore to me a hundredfold all I have wasted and lost. Blot out all mine iniquities in thy compassion, cover all my sins with thy charity, make amends for all my negligences by thy love, and in that love restore to me that liberty of spirit wherein thou, the true and sinless Heir, didst die for me, and set me at liberty at the cost of thine own Blood. Make me such as thou willest and desirest me to be, and in the hour of my death open to me the door of thy most benign and tender Heart, that through thee I may enter without impediment into the repose of thy thrilling love, and possess thee and enjoy thee, thou true Joy of my heart. Amen.

THREE PRAYERS FOR A PERSON IN THE AGONY OF DEATH

A certain Pope on his deathbed asked his chaplain to say these three prayers for him when he entered into his agony. This was done; and after his death he appeared and told him that all his sins had been effaced by Jesus through the virtue of these prayers, and that he had entered heaven with his Lord.

FIRST PRAYER

Lord have mercy.
Christ have mercy.
Lord have mercy.
Our Father. Hail Mary.

O LORD Jesus Christ, I beseech thee by thy own sacred Agony, and by the most fervent prayer thou didst pray in the Garden of Olives, when thy sweat became as it were drops of blood falling down upon the ground, that thou wouldst vouchsafe to offer and set forth before thy heavenly Father for the manifold sins of this sick person that dire sweat of Blood which the exceeding sorrow of thy · Heart wrung from thy Body. And do thou be pleased to deliver him in this hour of his death from all the anguish and punishment which he most justly fears that he has deserved by his sins. Amen.

SECOND PRAYER

Lord have mercy.
Christ have mercy.
Lord have mercy.
Our Father. Hail Mary.

O LORD Jesus Christ, who for the salvation of the world didst condescend to die upon thy hard cross, I beseech thee that thou wouldst vouchsafe to offer and set forth before thy heavenly Father for the sinful soul of this sick person all the bitterness thou didst endure thereon, and above all when thy most holy Soul went forth from thy blessed Body. And do thou be pleased to deliver him in this hour of his death from all the sufferings and torments which he most justly fears that he has deserved by his sins. Amen.

THIRD PRAYER

Lord have mercy.
Christ have mercy.
Lord have mercy.
Our Father. Hail Mary.

O LORD Jesus Christ, who hast said by thy prophet: Yea, I have loved thee with an everlasting love; therefore have I drawn thee, taking pity on thee: by the love which drew thee down from heaven to earth to bear all our woe and sorrow, I beseech thee that thou wouldst vouchsafe to offer and set forth that thy great love before thy heavenly Father for the soul of this sick person, and to deliver it from all the penalties and the woe which he most justly fears that he has deserved by his many sins. Be thou at hand to help him, O compassionate Jesus, now in this hour of his death; open to him the gate of life, and lead forth his soul into the Paradise of joy and exultation, that he may praise thee throughout eternity. Amen.

OFFERING OF THE PASSION OF CHRIST FOR THE FAITHFUL DEPARTED

LOOK down, O Father of compassion, from thy high and holy seat upon the hapless souls detained in purgatory. Look upon all the pains and torments wherewith they are so piteously chastised; regard now the plaintive groans and tears which they pour forth unto thee; hear the prayers and the supplications wherewith they entreat thy mercy, and be merciful unto their sins. Remember, O most compassionate Father, all the sufferings which thy Son hath endured for them; remember his precious Blood, shed in such abundance for them; call to mind the most bitter death which he suffered for them, and have mercy on them. For all the sins they have ever committed against thee I offer thee the most holy life and conversation of thy most beloved Son; for all their negligences I offer thee his most fervent desires towards thee; for all their omissions I offer thee the great abundance of his merits; for their every insult and wrong to thee I offer thee the sweet submission with which he honoured thee. Finally, for all the chastisements which they have ever incurred I offer thee all the mortifications, fastings, watchings, the labours and afflictions, wounds and stripes, passion and death, which he endured in such spotless innocence and with such loving eagerness; beseeching thee now to suffer thy anger to be appeased towards them, and to lead them forth into everlasting joy. Amen.

FOUR PRAYERS FOR THE DEPARTED

Written by St. Gertrude with the approval of our Lord.

When St. Gertrude was about to say these prayers together with the psalter, she asked our Lord whether they were acceptable to him, and received this answer: They are so acceptable to me that whenever a soul is liberated from purgatory, it is to me as though my own soul were delivered out of captivity, and I will surely reward them in due time, in the omnipotence of my boundless compassion. Wherefore, although you cannot recite the whole psalter, say at least these four most effectual prayers, and after each of them say:

HAIL, Jesus Christ, Splendour of the Father; hail, Prince of peace, Gate of heaven, living Bread, Offspring of the Virgin, Vessel of the Godhead.

V. Eternal rest grant unto them, O Lord.

R. And let perpetual light shine upon them.

Or, De profundis.

FIRST PRAYER

I ADORE, salute, and bless thee, O sweetest Lord Jesus Christ, and I praise thee and give thee thanks with the love of all thy creatures for the vast love wherewith thou didst condescend to be made man for us, to be born, to endure hunger and thirst, toils and sorrows, for thirty-three years, and to bestow on us Thyself in the most holy Sacrament; beseeching thee that thou wouldst vouchsafe to unite and blend with the merits of thy most holy conversation and life this my prayer, which I make to thee for the soul of N. departed [or, for the souls of all the faithful departed]; and to supply from the great abundance of those merits, and perfectly to complete whatsoever he has neglected in thy worship and love, in thanksgiving and in prayer, in virtue and good works, and all the service due to thee, in all that by thy grace he might have done and has not done, or did from impure motives, or carelessly and imperfectly. Amen.

SECOND PRAYER

I ADORE, salute, and bless thee, O sweetest Lord Jesus Christ, and I give thee thanks for that love wherewith thou, the Creator of all things, didst condescend for our redemption to be seized and bound and dragged away to judgment, to be trampled upon, buffeted and spit upon, to be scourged and crowned with thorns, to be condemned to bear thine own cross, to be stripped and nailed to the cross, to die a most bitter death and to be pierced through with the lance. And in union with that love I offer thee these my unworthy prayers, beseeching thee to blot out and efface utterly through the merits of thy most holy Passion and Death whatsoever this soul for which I pray has ever done against thy will, by evil thoughts or words or deeds; and that thou wouldst vouchsafe to offer to God the Father all the sorrow and the anguish of thy torn Body and of thy desolated Soul, all thy merits and all thine actions, for all that chastisement which he has incurred at the hands of thy justice. Amen.

THIRD PRAYER

I ADORE, salute, and bless thee, O sweetest Lord Jesus Christ, and I give thee thanks for all the love and the faithfulness with which thou didst overcome death and rise from the dead, and glorify our flesh by ascending in it to the right hand of the Father; beseeching thee that thou wouldst now vouchsafe to render the soul for which I pray partaker of thy triumph and of thy glory. Amen.

FOURTH PRAYER

I ADORE, salute, and bless thee, O sweetest Lord Jesus Christ, and I render thee thanks for all the graces thou hast ever bestowed on thy glorious Mother and on all thine elect, in union with the gratitude with which all thy saints exult in the bliss thou hast obtained for them through thy holy Incarnation, Passion, and Resurrection; beseeching thee that thou wouldst vouchsafe to supply to this soul from the merits and prayers of the same glorious Virgin and all thy saints, whatever is lacking to his own. Amen.

THE LORD'S PRAYER FOR THE DEPARTED

On one occasion when St. Mechtilde had received Holy Communion for the departed, our Lord appeared to her, saying: Recite for them one Our Father. *And as she prayed she received by divine inspiration the prayer which follows, the which when she had recited she saw a great multitude of souls ascending into heaven.*

OUR Father, *who art in heaven.* I beseech thee that thou wouldst forgive all the souls in purgatory, whereinsoever they have

neither loved nor worthily honoured thee, their
adorable and most beloved Father, who of
thine own mere grace didst adopt them to be
thy children, and have thrust thee forth from
their hearts in which thou didst delight to
dwell. And in satisfaction for this their sin,
I offer thee that love and honour which thy
beloved Son showed thee upon earth, and that
most abundant satisfaction which he hath made
for all their sins. Amen.

Hallowed be thy Name. I beseech thee, O
thou Father of compassion, forgive the souls
of the faithful departed whereinsoever they
have not worthily honoured nor duly made
mention of thy holy Name, but have taken it
in vain, and by their scandalous life rendered
themselves unworthy of the name of Christians.
And in satisfaction for these their sins I offer
thee the consummate holiness of thy Son,
whereby he magnified thy Name by his teaching, and made it honourable by his work.
Amen.

Thy kingdom come. I beseech thee, O
Father of compassion, vouchsafe to forgive
the souls of the faithful departed whereinsoever they have not fervently longed nor
ardently striven after thee and thy kingdom,
in which alone is true rest and abiding glory.
And for this and all their sloth in doing good
I offer thee the most holy and longing desires
of thy Son, wherewith he desired to make
them heirs together with him of his kingdom.
Amen.

Thy will be done on earth, as it is in heaven.
I beseech thee, O Father of compassion, vouchsafe to forgive the souls of the faithful departed, and especially of those consecrated to
thee in the religious life, whereinsoever they
have not preferred thy will above their own,
nor have loved it in all things, but have too
often lived and done only according to their
own will. And in satisfaction for this their
disobedience I offer thee the union of the sweetest Heart of thy Son with thy Will, and all
that his most ready and loving obedience
wherewith he was obedient unto thee, even to
the death of the cross. Amen.

Give us this day our daily bread. I beseech
thee, O Father of compassion, vouchsafe to
forgive the souls of the faithful departed
whereinsoever they have not received the most
blessed and adorable Sacrament of the Altar
with pure and perfect desire, devotion, and
love; or have received it unworthily, or seldom,
or not at all. And in satisfaction for these
their sins I offer thee the consummate holiness
and the devotion of thy Son, together with
that most ardent love and ineffable yearning
desire wherewith he bestowed upon us this
most inestimable treasure. Amen.

*And forgive us our trespasses, as we forgive
them that trespass against us.* I beseech thee,
O Father of compassion, vouchsafe to forgive
the souls of the faithful departed whereinsoever they have sinned against thee by any one

of the seven mortal sins, and especially wherein they have not forgiven those who had trespassed against them, or have not loved their enemies. And for all these their sins I offer thee that most sweet and tender prayer which thy Son prayed to thee for his enemies while hanging on the cross. Amen.

And lead us not into temptation. I beseech thee, O Father of compassion, vouchsafe to forgive the souls of the faithful departed whereinsoever they have not resisted their concupiscence and the sins to which they were especially prone, but have again and again consented to the devil and the flesh, and entangled themselves by their own will in many grievous evils. And for all these their manifold sins I offer thee the glorious victory wherewith thy Son overcame the world and the devil, together with all his most holy life and conversation, his toil and weariness, his most bitter Passion and his Death. Amen.

But deliver us and them *from* every *evil* and every woe through the merits of thy beloved Son, and bring us to the kingdom of thy glory, which is none other than thy most glorious self. Amen.

A SHORT AND EFFICACIOUS PRAYER FOR THE FAITHFUL DEPARTED

O MOST compassionate Jesus, have mercy on the souls detained in purgatory, for whose redemption thou didst take upon thee our nature and endure a bitter death. Mercifully hear their groanings, look with pity on the tears which they now shed before thee, and by the virtue of thy Passion release them from the pains due unto their sins. O most pitiful Jesus, let thy precious Blood reach down into purgatory, and refresh and revive the captive souls which suffer there. Stretch forth unto them thy strong right hand, and bring them forth into the place of refreshment, light, and peace. Amen.

PRAYER TO THE FAITHFUL DEPARTED

O MOST afflicted and unrepining souls, may Jesus Christ have mercy upon you, who for you was crucified and died, and may he refresh you in your sufferings by the sprinkling of his precious Blood. I commend you to that exceeding love which drew down the Son of God from heaven, and constrained him to a most bitter death on earth, that in that amazing compassion wherewith he entered into and took upon himself all the afflictions of the afflicted, he may have compassion on you. And for your full solace and refreshment I offer you all that filial love which the same Jesus Christ felt towards the Father in his Divinity, and towards Mary in his Humanity. Amen.

PRAYER IN A BURIAL-GROUND

HAIL., all ye faithful souls of Christ; may he give you rest, who is himself the one true Rest. May Jesus Christ, the Son of the living God, who for our salvation and for that of all mankind was born of the Immaculate Virgin and redeemed you with his precious Blood, bless you, release you from your pain, raise you up in the day of judgment, and place you with his holy angels. Amen.

PART IX

PRAYERS FOR FORGIVENESS OF SINS AND CONFESSION

Our Lord said to St. Gertrude: That you may be assured with what tender condescension I receive those who repent of their sins with true compunction of heart and a firm resolution to avoid all sin in future, know that my heart is touched with ineffable sweetness of delight whenever a sinner recalls to mind with true sorrow of heart that he has wandered far from me by the alienation of his heart, or by vain and idle words, or by sinful or useless actions. Whence it comes to pass that, whenever he remembers his sins, saying with true compunction of soul these or any like words: Alas, unhappy man that I am! how have I squandered and wasted the time in which I have not lived for thee, my Lord and my God, who hast so loved me! in the meekness and humbleness of my heart I take up his words, and set them forth before God the Father with a harmony so ravishing, drawn from the depths of my Divinity, that all the heavenly host of blessed spirits break forth into joyous song. And thus it is that there is such joy in heaven upon one sinner that doth penance. And whenever I bring forth any faithful soul through the gate of death into the heavenly court, besides the endearments with which I enchant his disenthralled soul all along that wondrous way, I shed upon him all the joy which I, together with all the heavenly host, have felt whenever with true compunction of heart he has done penance on earth.

ACCUSATION OF HIMSELF BY ONE WHO HAS GRIEVOUSLY SINNED

O ALMIGHTY and eternal God, behold I, a miserable, unworthy, and faithless sinner, so often and in such manifold ways a rebel and ungrateful to thee, come unto thee, my Creator and my Redeemer, accusing myself and confessing before thee all my abominations and many crimes. In the spirit of humiliation and with truly contrite heart I confess before thee that I have many times blasphemed thy holy Name, and transgressed thy just commandments, and set at naught thy will, and rendered vain all thy gifts and all thy work within me, and polluted my whole soul and my body, and perverted to thy dishonour thy graces and thy benefits, and offended thee in numberless ways by my sins and my iniquities. And, alas, I have too long and too stubbornly continued in these most grievous and heinous sins, in this malice and perfidy, abusing thy tenderness, leading my heart astray, and defiling all my soul. And I have not only drawn away from thee my own soul, but many other souls which thou hast purchased with thy most Precious Blood, and which I have led from thee by evil example and persuasion, and given over to the devil to be slain. Behold, O Lord my God, thy wicked enemy lies prostrate at thy feet; behold in thy power this perverse and recreant sinner, who of his own accord gives himself up unto thee. Do with me whatsoever seemeth good to thee; for with resolved will I submit myself to the rigour of thy justice, prepared to endure whatever vengeance thou willest to exact from me; only, do thou show thy mercy on me, and receive me into thy favour. For art thou not my Father, whose compassion knoweth no bounds, whose loving-kindnesses are infinite? And although I have rendered myself unworthy to be called thy son, yet do I acknowledge no other Father than thee alone. Wherefore I cast myself at the feet of thy mercy, and implore thee, by thine omnipotence, by thy wisdom and thy goodness, to pardon and forgive my most grievous sins. Receive me now once more to thy favour, O thou sweet Jesus, Son of the living God, who art appointed our advocate, the one mediator between us and thy Father. I beseech thee by that charity which drew thee down from heaven into the Virgin's womb, and constrained thee thence to the passion and ignominy of the Cross; I beseech thee by all the scorn and insult heaped upon thee, by each one of the drops of thy most precious Blood shed for us; obtain for me the pardon of all my sins, and reconcile me fully with thy Father. Amen.

ANOTHER SELF-ACCUSATION OF A SINNER

O LORD my God, thou unfathomable abyss of compassion, my sins are more in number than the sand upon the seashore, and I am not worthy to lift mine eyes up towards thee. My soul is a loathsome sink of iniquities, a foul and festering carcase of corruptions. Mine iniquities are gone over my head, and as a heavy burden have become heavy upon me. Within me reigns unchecked pride, vain-glory, impurity, avarice, envy, gluttony, sloth, and all kinds of evil. What shall I do, wretch that I am, or where hide myself from the face of the anger of God? Alas, O my Lord God, how many are my wounds, how utter the weakness of my soul. To whom shall I pour out my complaint by reason of all my evil and my sin, but unto thee, O Lord, thou Saviour and Redeemer of my soul? O Jesus, Son of the living God, have mercy upon me, for with thee nothing is impossible, save to refuse mercy to the wretched. O sweet Jesus, restore to me thy grace once more, and receive me to thy friendship. Look upon me, not according to my merits, but according to thy great goodness. I grieve exceedingly for all the sins whereby I have offended thee, my most kind and loving God. O Lord my God, I hate, I abhor, I detest and abominate all my sins even

as thou dost execrate and abhor them; would
that I could grieve for them as thou dost desire. And to supply what is lacking in my
grief, I offer thee all that contrition, all that
sorrow, all that aversion from sin, which thy
Son felt and endured in the Garden of Olives,
when by reason of his excessive sorrow and
anguish of soul his sweat fell in drops of
Blood to the ground, and all his bowels were
troubled within him; beseeching thee that thou
wouldst now vouchsafe to accept that contrition in supply of what is lacking to mine,
and to absolve me from my sins. Amen.

ACT OF TRUE CONTRITION

The doctors of the Church teach that if a sin-
ner feels such sorrow for his sins that he is
prepared to submit willingly to all the punish-
ment they have deserved, he thereby becomes
reconciled to God, and all his punishment is
remitted.

O MOST gracious God, I most unworthy of
thy creatures have offended thy Divine
goodness in such manifold ways, of my own
mere malice and perversity, that thou mightest
justly abhor me, and pursue me as thy stub-
born and most inveterate enemy. O Christ
Jesus, I confess that I have dealt wickedly and
have done exceeding evil in thy sight; but I
grieve for my sins with so deep and lively a
sorrow, that I would rather endure any ill than

sin against thee henceforward by even one mortal sin. Nor do I grieve because of the dread and exceeding punishment I have deserved, but because I have so heinously and so unjustly offended against thee, my loving, kind, and faithful God, who hast never done me the least ill or injustice, but hast bestowed on me all manner of good things. Pardon me, O most merciful Jesus, for the sake of that love wherewith thou didst pray to thy Father for thy murderers; for I profess my readiness to make a true and condign satisfaction to thee for every insult wherewith I have provoked thee by my sins. I do not ask thee to remit to me the pains I have deserved; but I am most ready to accept them as chastisements from thy fatherly hand, when and how and where it shall seem good to thee, and the glory of thy justice shall require. Wherefore I submit myself unto thee with the most profound humility and resignation, and I embrace with all my heart thy just judgment upon me, and gladly welcome whatever adversities and evils thou shalt lay upon me in time or in eternity. Amen.

SHORT CONFESSION OF SINS

When St. Gertrude had on one occasion made this confession of her sins, she appeared cleansed from every spot of sin, and whiter than the driven snow.

BEHOLD, O my Lord, I an unworthy sinner confess with sorrow that I have many times sinned against thy divine omnipotence through human frailty, and have in many ways offended against thy divine wisdom through my ignorance, and through my malice have rendered vain all thy priceless goodness towards me. Wherefore, O Father of mercies, have mercy on me; and give me strength from thine omnipotence to resist all things which are contrary to thee, from thine unsearchable wisdom give me prudence to detect and avoid whatsoever may offend thy pure eyes, and of thine overflowing compassion grant me to cleave to thee with such constant fidelity that I may never, in any the least point, swerve from thy adorable will.

PETITION TO JESUS

That he would deign himself to expiate our transgressions by his own most holy life and conversation.

O MOST compassionate Jesus, full of pity and of mercy, who despisest not the sighing of the wretched; alas, my whole life is perished and gone without fruit, nor have I ever done any thing good in thy sight. To thee therefore I betake myself, imploring thy clemency. Do thou speak for me, do thou satisfy for me. Wash away all the defilement of my sinful eyes with the pure tears of thy

most glorious eyes. By the sweet compassion
of thy blessed ears take away all the iniquity
of my sinful ears. By the pure intention of
thy most holy thoughts and by the ardent love
of thy pierced heart, wash away all the guilt
of my evil thoughts and of my wicked heart.
By the thrilling power of the sweet words of
thy blessed mouth, blot out all the offences of
my polluted mouth. By the perfection of thy
actions and the crucifixion of thy hands, wash
away all the offences of my impious hands.
By the painful weariness of thy blessed feet,
and by their cruel piercing with the nails,
wash away all the defilement of my sinful
feet. By the majestic innocence of thy life,
and by thy unblemished holiness, wash away
the foulness of my corrupt life. Finally, do
thou wash away, efface, extinguish all the
sins of my heart and my soul in the abundant
streams of thy most precious Blood, that so
by thy most holy merits I may be thoroughly
cleansed, and henceforward keep all thy commandments blameless. Amen.

A DEVOUT PRAYER FOR PARDON THROUGH THE
PASSION OF CHRIST

I ADORE and bless thee, O most gentle Lord
Jesus, as thou hangest on the tree of the
cross, and pourest out thy roseate Blood in expiation of the sins of the world. I accuse myself now with sincere contrition of heart of

the manifold insults and infidelities whereby I have grieved thee. O good Jesus, I confess that by reason of my vile and shameful sins I am the cause of thy passion and death, and that in thy passion my sins were more grievous to thee than the buffetings and the stripes of the rude soldiers. To thee, therefore, I confess and acknowledge my malice and my iniquity, and I prostrate myself before thy cross, in the spirit of humiliation, imploring thy forgiveness. I cast all my iniquities and my sins into the depths of thy mercy and clemency, and into those bleeding wounds which thou didst receive for my salvation; beseeching thee that thou wouldst so wash them away and efface them with thy most precious Blood and the all-cleansing water from thy sacred Side, that thou mayest remember them no more for ever. In perfect expiation and satisfaction for all the sins which I have committed by thought, desire, and the perverse affections of my heart, I offer to thine eternal Father thy immaculate Heart with all the treasures it contains. And for all the vain and hurtful words my lips have spoken, do thou set forth before him all the words which issued from thy most sacred mouth. And for all the sinful deeds which my hands have done, show him thy pierced Hands, and so appease thy Father with thy unspotted innocence, that through thee I may now obtain forgiveness of all my crimes. And to this end I offer thee that ineffable sweetness of delight which one divine person communicates to another in the most adorable Trinity. Amen.

A PRAYER FOR PARDON

(*St. Gertrude*)

O LORD Jesus Christ, thou overflowing Fountain of all mercy, behold, I thy wretched and unhappy creature return once more to thee, and accuse myself in the bitterness of my soul that I have not kept my resolutions, but have again fallen into my former sins; that I have served thee with extreme negligence, and have been lukewarm and careless in my devotion to thee and love of thee; that I have too much entangled myself in vain and transitory things, and have far too eagerly sought earthly and hurtful pleasures; and that in these and innumerable other ways I have many times offended thee, the sweetest Spouse of my soul. And although thine essential blessedness, O my God, can neither be increased nor diminished, because thou canst have no need of me or of my goods, nevertheless my sinful and careless life does in some sort tend to the notable prejudice of thy honour and glory. Thou knowest, O my God, what sorrow I now have, or at least what sorrow I ought to have, in my heart for all these my sins. Wherefore, O most tender Father, I confess to thee with most bitter contrition of heart all those sins whereof thou knowest me to be guilty; most humbly beseeching thee that thou wouldst supply whereinsoever I have failed through malice, or wickedness, or carelessness, from the treasures of that mighty love, the fulness of which rests on him who now sitteth at thy right hand, bone of my bone, and flesh of my flesh. For it is through him, in the power of the Holy Ghost, in union with his princely compassion, humility, and reverence, and in the measure of the power thou hast given us; it is through him that I pour forth before thee my lamentation and my complaint, by reason of my exceeding misery and grief for having so often offended thy divine munificent goodness in thought, in word, and in deed. I offer and set forth before thee now, in satisfaction for all my negligences and for the blotting out of all my iniquities, that surpassing prayer of thy most beloved Son, that prayer rendered so fervent by the anguish which wrung from him his sweat of blood, so devout by the purity and simplicity of his innocence, and so availing by the glowing love of his Divinity. Amen.

PRAYER BEFORE CONFESSION

O SWEETEST Jesus, who in thy loving desire for our salvation hast instituted the Sacrament of confession for the consolation of all sinners, that by its virtue we might be cleansed from all our iniquities, and recover the grace we have lost; behold me, a most wretched sinner, who have offended thee again by many sins, and defiled my soul with many stains, now come back once more to thee; resolving to receive this most munificent sacrament with most steadfast hope and confidence that thou wilt grant me remission of all my sins; and to accuse myself with most profound humility and contrition of soul before the priest, thy representative, of all and each of my sins, in so far as I can recall them to my mind; nor will I knowingly hide any mortal sin, however vile and shameful it be. And I desire to include in this my confession, all those sins which I cannot now recall to my memory, and all my venial sins; and I confess them all to thee as to my great High Priest high over all; and in presence of all the court of heaven I avow and proclaim myself a perfidious wretch and traitor against thine adorable Majesty. I beseech thee therefore, O most merciful Father, that thou wouldst vouchsafe to look on me a miserable sinner with that eye of compassion wherewith thou didst look upon thy Son when he fell on his face in the Garden of Olives, crushed to the earth by the sins of all mankind, and graciously to hear me while I implore thy pardon. And to supply what is lacking to my most imperfect contrition, I offer thee all that overwhelming grief which thine only-begotten Son endured throughout his whole life on earth in his sweetest Heart by reason of the sins of the world, and especially when in the Garden of Olives the extremity of his anguish wrung from him his sweat of blood; beseeching thee that thou wouldst cleanse my soul from all its defilements in the stream of that most holy Blood, and adorn it with a purity whiter than snow. Amen.

SHORT AND EFFICACIOUS ACT OF CONTRITION

(St. Mechtilde)

O SWEET Jesus, I grieve for my sins; vouchsafe to supply whatever is lacking to my true sorrow, and to offer for me to God the Father all the grief which thou hast endured because of my sins and those of the whole world. Amen.

As you enter the confessional, say:

BEHOLD, O Lord, I a vile sinner, poor and guilty and unworthy, come unto thee, the overflowing abyss of compassion, that I may be washed from every stain and cleansed from every sin. Amen.

After Confession, say the following, from Psalm 102.

BLESS the Lord, O my soul: and let all that is within me bless his holy Name.

Bless the Lord, O my soul: and forget not all he hath done for thee.

Who forgiveth all thine iniquities: who healeth all thy diseases.

Who redeemeth thy life from destruction: who crowneth thee with mercy and compassion.

The Lord is compassionate and merciful: long-suffering and plenteous in mercy.

He hath not dealt with us according to our sins: nor rewarded us according to our iniquities.

As far as the east is from the west: so far hath he removed our iniquities from us.

As a father hath compassion on his children: so hath the Lord compassion on them that fear him.

For he knoweth our frame: he remembereth that we are but dust.

Bless the Lord, all his angels: ye ministers of his that do his will.

Bless the Lord, all his works in every place of his dominion: bless thou the Lord, O my soul.

Let us pray

O ALMIGHTY and merciful God, whose mercy is boundless and everlasting, and the riches of thy goodness infinite, I give thanks with all my mind and my heart for the most amazing and exceeding goodness which thou hast now shown me, in that thou hast so graciously pardoned all my sins, and restored me to thy grace and favour. Blessed be thy Divine compassion, O my God, and blessed by the incomprehensible love of thy beloved Son, which constrained him to institute so gentle and so mighty a remedy for our sins. Wherefore in union with all the thanksgivings which have ever ascended to thee from truly penitent hearts I sing aloud thy glad praises, on behalf of all in heaven, on earth, and in purgatory, for ever and ever. Amen.

PRAYER BEFORE PERFORMING SACRAMENTAL PENANCE

AND since I have so grievously insulted thee, O most tender and loving God, by my manifold sins and negligences, I am ready now to make perfect satisfaction to thy divine justice to the utmost of my ability. To this end I will faithfully and most reverently perform the penance appointed me by my confessor in thy name; and would that I could perform it with so great devotion and love as to give thee an honour and delight greater than the insult and outrage of my sins! And that this may be so, I unite and blend this my penance with all the works of satisfaction which thy beloved Son accomplished during the three-and-thirty years of his life on earth, and in union with his fastings, his watchings, and his prayers, I offer thee this my penance and my prayer. Look, therefore, O most loving Father, on me thy most bounden debtor, now prostrate at thy feet, desiring to make thee adequate satisfaction and reparation for all the insults and injuries I have done thee; and grant me strength and grace to say this prayer according to thy most holy will. Amen.

Here perform your sacramental penance and then say as follows:

O MOST holy Father, I offer thee this my confession and my satisfaction in union with all the acts of penance which have ever been done to the glory of thy holy Name; beseeching thee that thou wouldst vouchsafe to accept it, and to render it availing through the merits of the passion of thy beloved Son, and through the intercession of the ever-blessed Virgin Mary, and of all thy holy Apostles, Martyrs, Confessors, and Virgins. Whatever has been lacking to me in sincere and earnest preparation, in perfect contrition, in frank and clear confession, I commend to the most loving Heart of thine only-begotten Son, that treasury of all good and of all grace, from whose overflowing abundance all debts to thee are fully acquitted; that through it all my negligences and defects in the reception of this holy Sacrament may be fully and perfectly supplied to thine everlasting praise and glory, and that thou mayest effectually absolve me in heaven, even as thy minister has with thy authority absolved me here on earth: through Jesus Christ our Lord, who liveth and reigneth with thee and the Holy Ghost, ever world without end. Amen.

PRAYER TO BE SAID BY A PRIEST BEFORE
ADMINISTERING THE SACRAMENT OF
PENANCE

O LORD Jesus, I desire and intend to administer this holy sacrament of penance in union with that all-transcending love wherewith thou didst sanctify it, when, constrained by thine eager desire of our salvation, thou didst institute it and appoint it to be administered by thy Apostles and by their successors, for the glory of thy holy name and the salvation of the whole human race, beseeching thee that through thy unspeakable love, it may work in me, and in those to whom I shall now administer it, increase of salvation and of everlasting blessedness. May the grace of the holy Spirit so enlighten, inflame and guard my senses that I may be enabled to discharge this my commanded ministry; according to thy adorable will, and be fortified and defended against every assault of temptation. In the name of the Father, and of the Son, and of the Holy Ghost. Amen.

PRAYER AFTER ADMINISTERING THE SACRAMENT
OF PENANCE

O LORD Jesus Christ, Son of the living God, receive this my bounden service and ministry with that transcending love wherewith thou didst absolve the Blessed Mary Magdalene, and all sinners who fled for refuge unto thee.

And whereinsoever I have failed in the administration of this holy sacrament through my negligence or imperfection, do thou deign to satisfy for me and supply all my defects. I commend to thy sweetest heart all and each of those who have now confessed their sins to me, beseeching thee to keep them evermore, to preserve them from falling back again into sin, and after this miserable life to bring them to thine everlasting joy.   Amen.

PART X
PRAYERS FOR HOLY COMMUNION

PREPARATION FOR COMMUNION

O MOST sweet and loving Jesus, I the most unworthy of all thy creatures propose now to receive the most holy sacrament of thy Body and Blood, as the most effectual remedy for all my miseries of body and of soul; with most certain confidence and with most steadfast faith that I shall thus not only obtain the supply of all my need, but also most perfectly please thy supreme Majesty and all the inhabitants of heaven. But, O thou supreme and ineffable Majesty, before whose face the heavens are not clean and its strong pillars tremble, how shall I, a vile worm of the earth, a very sink of all most loathsome corruption and misery, dare to receive thee, who art the Fountain and Source of all purity, into my polluted heart? How shall I presume to receive thee into a heart all set around with briars and thorns, reeking with the foul vapours of carnal and worldly lusts? Wherefore, O thou most compassionate Lover of my soul, I blush exceedingly and am confounded before thee, and quake with fear lest I should outrage thee by receiving thee into an abode so foul, so unworthy of thy Majesty. But, O most merciful Jesus, who hast said with thy gracious lips that they that are whole need not the physician, but they that are sick, who didst invite the blind and the lame, the poor and the needy, to thy supper; behold, as one of them, yea, as the poorest and most wretched of them all, I will draw near to the most sacred feast of thy Body and Blood, not in presumption, but with lowly confidence.

(From S. Gertrude)

FOR the love of thee I bitterly grieve for all and every one of my sins and my negligences, whereby I have ever offended and grieved thy most tender loving kindness and polluted my soul with such loathsome defilement. O would that I could change the whole sea into blood, and that I could pour its mighty flood through my head and my heart, that thus that sink of unutterable abominations might be cleansed, which thou, my last End, hast chosen for thine habitation. O would that my heart could be torn from my body and purified in fiercest fire from all its dross, that thus it might offer thee an abode, not, alas, worthy of thee, but at least not so utterly unworthy. But why do I disquiet my soul within me, seeing that even if a thousand years were given me I could not prepare myself to receive thee befittingly; for of myself I have nothing whatever which could in any way avail towards so august and solemn a preparation as beseems thy adorable Majesty. Wherefore, O most loving Jesus, I cast myself in the dust before thee in the humility of my heart, and I beseech thy clemency to deign so to prepare me that I may partake of this heavenly banquet to thy glory and to the profit of all the whole world. I offer and abandon to thy tender pity all my substance, all that I am and all I have, earnestly desiring and beseeching thee that thou wouldst thyself vouchsafe to prepare within me all that is most pleasing to thy divine goodness. I offer and abandon to thee, O thou surpassingly sweet Lover of my soul, my whole heart, beseeching thee that thou wouldst wash it in that water of mighty efficacy which flowed from thy most holy Side, and adorn it for thine indwelling with the precious Blood of thy most sacred Heart, and fit it for thyself with the fragrant incense of thy divine love. Amen.

O ALL ye Saints of God, and ye especially, my most beloved patrons, I salute and venerate you with the most profound affection of my heart, I adore and bless the infinite goodness and condescension of the ever-adorable Trinity for all the grace which has ever flowed forth from that unfathomable overflowing abyss for your salvation; beseeching you all in general and each one of you in particular, that you would deign to offer in sacrifice to the bright and ever-peaceful Trinity, in satisfaction for all my negligence and unworthiness, all that fervent zeal and preparedness with which you stood perfect and consummate in the presence of the glory of God on the day of your entrance into heaven, to receive your everlasting reward.

To obtain this grace say with St. Gertrude the Psalm: Laudate Dominum, omnes gentes.

TO THE BLESSED VIRGIN

The blessed Virgin herself taught St. Gertrude these prayers, assuring her that by their virtue she would draw down upon herself the blessing of the holy Trinity.

O MOST chaste Virgin Mary, I beseech thee by that unspotted purity wherewith thou didst prepare for the Son of God a dwelling of delights in thy virginal womb, that by the intercession I may be cleansed from every stain.

O most humble Virgin Mary, I beseech thee by that most profound humility whereby thou didst merit to be raised high above all the choirs of angels and of saints, that by thy intercession all my negligences may be expiated.

O most amiable Virgin Mary, I beseech thee, by that ineffable love which united thee so closely and so inseparably to God, that by thy intercession I may obtain an abundance of all merits.   Amen.

PRAYER TO OUR DIVINE LORD

St. Gertrude, having recited this prayer before communion, sought to know what she had gained by it, and received this answer from our Lord: Thou hast gained this, that thou dost now appear before the inhabitants of heaven arrayed in those ornaments which thou didst ask of me.

O MOST loving Lord Jesus Christ, I beseech thee, by all the love of thy sweetest Heart, that thou wouldst vouchsafe to offer for me all that perfection wherewith thou didst stand arrayed in the presence of God the Father when thou didst ascend on high to enter into thy glory; and through thy sinless and unspotted manhood to render my polluted soul pure and free from every sin, and through thy most glorious Divinity to endow and adorn it with every virtue, and through the virtue of that love, which has for ever united thy supreme Divinity to thine immaculate Humanity, to furnish it befittingly with thy best gifts. Amen.

PRAYER BEFORE COMMUNION

When you are about to receive holy communion, follow the counsel which our Lord gave to St. Mechtilde, saying: When you approach to receive me, receive me with the intention of feeling all the glowing desire and love with which the heart of man has ever been inflamed. And I will accept this love, not as it is in thee, but as if it were what you desire it to be.

O JESUS most ardently desired and longed-for, behold the moment draws near, the rapturous moment in which I shall receive thee my God into my soul. Behold, O my Jesus, I come unto thee, and run to meet thee with the utmost devotion and reverence of which I am capable. Stretch forth, therefore, thy most sacred Hands to embrace my soul, those very pierced Hands of thine which thou didst stretch forth amidst the anguish of thy Passion to embrace all sinners. O my crucified Jesus, I stretch forth not my hands only, but my heart and my soul, to embrace thee and to lead thee into the most inner and secret recess of my heart. Oh, would that I had within me such and so great devotion, such and so great love, such and so great purity, as heart of man has been ever adorned withal! Would that I were filled with all virtues, with all holy desires, with perfect and consummate devotion. Would that I had the purity of all thine angels, the charity of all thine apostles, the holiness of all confessors, the chastity and cleanness of heart of all virgins! Would that I could receive thee now with all that devotion, reverence, and love wherewith thy most blessed Mother received thee in thine Incarnation, and in thine adorable Sacrament! Oh, would that I had thy own sacred and divine Heart, that I might therein receive thee as becomes thy ineffable Majesty!

O sweetest Jesus, I offer thee for my fitting preparation, and to make amends for all my unworthiness and all my negligences, all the preparation of heart, the devotion, the affections, the love wherewith all thy saints, and above all thy most blessed Mother, have ever received thee in this holy Sacrament. I offer thee, O most holy Jesus, thine own transcendently meritorious Heart, and all the ineffable virtues and graces which the most blessed Trinity bestowed without measure upon it, that therewith all my vileness and all my unworthiness may be covered, and that a befitting and most peaceful abode may be prepared for thee in my soul. Amen.

INVITATION TO JESUS

O JESUS surpassingly sweet, who hast said with thine own gracious lips that thy delights are to be with the children of men, my soul longeth for thee, my heart yearneth now towards thee. Wherefore I invite thee to come unto me with all that devotion and that love wherewith any loving soul hath ever invited thee to itself. Come, then, O most beloved Spouse of my soul; come, O most beloved and only Love of my soul; come and turn aside awhile into the poor and wretched hovel of my heart. Come, thou heavenly Physician, come and heal my stricken soul. Come, O Friend, a thousandfold above all others beloved, come and enrich my utter poverty.

Come, thou bright and genial Sun, and scatter the thick darkness which hangs upon my heart. Come, thou sweetest Manna, and satisfy my soul's exceeding hunger. Come, O Jesus, incomparable in thy loveliness; come, thou beloved of my heart's vows; come and sup with me in the vile chamber of my heart. And although I have made ready nothing which may beseem thy dazzling magnificence, yet wilt thou find therein one dish of savoury meat such as thou lovest a will which tends to thee alone, and affections wholly thine.

O thou my only Love, I long for thy coming with most eager desire, I await thy coming with yearning love. O thou fairest of the sons of men, O spring of inexhaustible sweetness, O thou sweeter than all sweetest delights, come, O come unto me, and disdain not thy poor and needy servant. Amen.

Here kiss the crucifix, and say with St. Gertrude:

O MOST loving Jesus, I embrace thee with the profoundest love of my heart, and in union with all the love of the prayers which ever flowed forth from thy sweetest lips, I beseech thee that thou wouldst deign to turn aside into the mean and wretched inn of my heart.

As you draw near to the holy table, repeat the words which our Lord taught to St. Gertrude:

BEHOLD, O Lord, I, a vile sinner, poor and guilty and unworthy, come unto thee, the overflowing abyss of compassion, that I may be washed from every stain and filled with every grace.

Say the following words with great fervour; for our Lord revealed to St. Gertrude that no one who draws near to holy communion with these dispositions can ever receive him with irreverence.

AND although I know myself to be a most utterly unworthy, an execrable and most abominable sinner, yet, trusting in thine ineffable compassion, I draw near to this most holy participation of thy Body and Blood with this firm intention, that for thy love and thy glory I should deem it a light thing to receive in this Sacrament the sentence of my eternal condemnation, were that possible, if the glory of thy divine compassion in not disdaining to give thyself to me might thereby shine forth with the greater splendour.

As you kneel to receive communion, cease not to sigh and long for your Beloved, saying:

COME, good Jesus, come, thou Spouse of my soul, come into my heart with that love with which thou didst enter into the Virgin's womb, &c.

AFTER COMMUNION

O GOOD Jesus, O sweet Jesus, O Jesus most lovely, O Jesus my only salvation and my consolation; and whence is this to me that thou shouldst come unto me, and not abhor to enter into my most polluted heart, defiled as it is with such exceeding stains and sins? Blessed be thy coming unto me, and blessed the sweetness of the love which hath constrained thee to visit me, thy poor and worthless creature. I cast myself now in the very dust before thy Face with the most profound humility and due reverence, and I kiss thy most sacred Feet, and adore thee, and I most humbly beseech thee that thou wouldst forgive me for having received thee, my Lord, with so great negligence, distraction, and lack of devotion. [*A priest may add:* for having stood at thine altar and touched and handled thee with so little reverence, and for having received, &c.]

Pardon me, O most tender Jesus, and through thy life-giving death blot out my great iniquity, and vouchsafe thyself to supply all my defects and satisfy for all my negligences. Wherefore, I beseech thee, deign to receive this my communion [*or,* this my sacrifice and communion] into thy sacred Heart, and offer it to God the Father with all the love and all the availingness with which thou didst offer thyself upon the cross.

And now, O good Jesus, I offer and make over to thee my most unworthy heart, beseeching thee that thou wouldst wash it in that most precious water which thy divine love caused to gush forth from thy sweetest Heart, fairer and more fragrant than the rose, glowing as a furnace with the ardour of thy love; and that thou wouldst sprinkle and revive it with the sweetest wine of thy most sacred Blood, pressed from thy divine Heart, as from a cluster of ripe grapes in the wine-press of thy cross. Amen.

OFFERING TO GOD THE FATHER, OF EXCEEDING EFFICACY

O MOST holy Father, behold, I thy most unworthy servant, trusting only in thine ineffable compassion, have received thy beloved Son our Lord Jesus Christ, and even now hold him in my heart as my own possession, most intimately united with me. Wherefore, receiving this thy Son into my arms, even as did holy Simeon, I offer him to thee with all that love and that fulness of intention wherewith he offered himself to thee for thine everlasting glory, while lying in the manger, and when he was hanging upon the cross. Look, O compassionate Father, on this offering, which I thine unworthy servant make to thee my living and true God, to thine everlasting praise and glory, for thine infinite rejoicing and delight.

I offer to thee the same, thy Son, for myself, and for all those for whom I am accustomed or bound to pray, in thanksgiving for all the benefits thou hast bestowed on us, and in supply of all those virtues and good works which, of our own mere negligence, we have failed to practise. I offer him to thee to obtain thy grace and thy mercy, that we may be preserved and delivered from all evil and sin, succoured in every necessity of body or of soul, and brought forth through a happy death into everlasting joys. Finally, I offer him to thee for the remission of all my sins, and in satisfaction for that huge debt which I cannot pay thee, seeing that it far exceeds even ten thousand talents; and therefore, casting myself at thy feet, O most merciful Father, I acknowledge and plead my utter poverty, in union with the bitterness of the passion of thy most sinless Son, in whom thou hast declared thyself well-pleased; and in and through him I make thee full reparation and satisfaction for my sins, offering thee all his sorrows, griefs, and tears, and all that expiation which he made upon the cross for the sins of the whole world.

Remember also, O Lord, thy servants who have gone before us with the sign of faith, and sleep the sleep of peace: for all and each of whom [and especially for N.] I offer thee that saving Victim whom I have now received, the Body and Blood of thy beloved Son; beseeching thee, that through his infinite dignity and worth, and through the merits of all saints, thou wouldst grant them pardon of all their sins, and merciful release from all their pains. Amen.

OFFERING TO THE SAINTS

You may form an idea of the efficacy of this offering from the vision vouchsafed to St. Gertrude when she had offered this Sacrament in honour of the holy angels; she saw these blessed spirits entranced with joy and gladness and overflowing with abundant and thrilling delights, as though they had never known bliss before.

O MOST blessed Virgin Mary, behold, I most humbly and lovingly set before thee thy Son, whom thou didst conceive in thy spotless womb, didst bring forth, and nourish at thy breasts, and press to thy heart with most tender and thrilling embraces; him in whose countenance thou didst ever joy, and find ever fresh delights, and who has this day given himself to me in the ineffable condescension of his divine love. I offer him to thee that thou mayest fold him in thine arms, and kiss him with the kisses of thy mouth, and love and worship him for me and together with me, and offer him, in deepest adoration, to the most Holy Trinity for my sins and the sins of all the world; so that the prerogative of thy great dignity may obtain for me what I dare not presume to hope of myself.

O all ye Saints of God, and ye especially my most beloved patrons, behold Jesus Christ, your Lord and Spouse, whom while ye lived in the flesh ye loved with all your heart and all your strength; for in and through him whom I have now received in the most holy Sacrament, I salute you all and each of you, and offer him to you for the signal increase of your joy, your glory and your blessedness, with all the love and the faithfulness which he showed you in time, and now showeth you evermore in eternity, beseeching you all to worship and adore him for me, and to offer him to the most Holy Trinity with all your consummate devotion on behalf of my necessities and those of the whole Church, and in thanksgiving for all the benefits he has ever bestowed upon me. And whatever I am unable to obtain of myself, do you impetrate for me, through your merits and intercessions. Amen.

THANKSGIVING

LET my heart and my soul, together with all the whole substance of my flesh, all my senses, and all my powers of mind and body give praise and thanks to thee, O sweetest Jesus, in union with all the creatures of thy hand, for the condescending mercy which thou, O most faithful Lover of our salvation, hast deigned to show me, most unworthy, in this sacred banquet of thy Body and Blood. O my sweetest God, were all the moments of my life uninterrupted acts of thanksgiving to thee, yet could I not answer or render thee for one of a thousand. Wherefore, acknowledging my utter insufficiency, I offer unto thee, O most blessed Trinity, all the praises and thanksgivings which the most sacred Humanity of our Lord Jesus Christ rendered thee throughout his whole earthly life, and especially when he instituted this Sacrament. Receive also, O compassionate Father, all those thanksgivings which the blessed Virgin Mary and all thy Saints have ever rendered thee with all their heart and all their soul, and especially when they have received this Sacrament; and mercifully grant that all my insufficiencies and my negligences may be supplied and satisfied for by their abundance and perfection. Amen.

A MOST EFFICACIOUS CONCLUSION

(*St. Gertrude*)

WHEREFORE, O Christ Jesus, in union with that all-transcending love wherewith thou didst most gratefully refer back to their unfathomable source all those streams which flowed forth from the Divinity upon thy deified Humanity, I offer thee, with the love of the whole universe of thy creatures, this most holy Sacrament, which the all-powerful sweetness of thine unsearchable Divinity drew forth from the depth of thy loving Heart, and which thou hast now vouchsafed to impart to me: beseeching thee, with the affections and the yearning desire of all creatures, that thou wouldst draw up this holy Sacrament and communion into thyself through the love of thy good and gentle

Spirit, that it may render thee that eternal, immense, unceasing, unfaltering praise which thy inscrutable wisdom knoweth to beseem the transcendent majesty of God the Father, and to gladden and rejoice the goodness of thine unutterably gracious Spirit: that it may be to thee a full and adequate thanksgiving for all the good and all the grace which thou hast ever wrought, or shalt ever hereafter work, in the hearts and souls of those who duly receive this divine Sacrament: that it may make thee full reparation and satisfaction for all things wherein my careless preparation, my feeble desire, or my languid devotion have impaired its effect within me: and lastly, that it may give thee highest praise and thanks for that thine incomprehensible goodness hath deigned to admit me, a vile worm of earth, to this royal banquet of heavenly delights. And seeing that my nothingness can make thee no return for this thine unimaginable goodness, I offer to thee now thy sweetest Heart, with all that fulless of gratitude and manifold and consummate blessedness which render it supremely, transcendently, for ever, and alone worthy of thee. Amen.

THREE PRAYERS FOR GAINING PLENARY
INDULGENCES

To gain a plenary indulgence, it is not enough to go to confession and communion; it is moreover necessary to visit some church, and to pray for the exaltation of the holy Church, for the rooting out of all heresies, and for concord and peace among Christian princes. To these ends you may use the following prayers.

FIRST PRAYER, FOR THE HOLY CHURCH

O MOST tender Lord Jesus Christ, who hast chosen the holy Church to thyself to be thy bride, and hast so loved it as to pour out thy life and thy blood for it; we implore thy clemency that thou wouldst deign to give it peace, to guard it, to unite it, and to govern it throughout the whole earth. Behold, O most merciful Jesus, with what unresting pertinacity it is assailed by its enemies. See with what appalling rage the gates of hell rise up against it. Suffer them not to prevail against it, I beseech thee: but keep and defend it with thy strong right arm. Behold, O most compassionate Jesus, how carelessly, and with what unseemly dishonour, thy divine worship is celebrated, how thy service is despised, and how little knowledge there is of thee upon earth. Send forth, therefore, fervent and unwearied labourers into thy harvest, that they may increase it, further it, and gather it into thy garner. Grant unto all the faithful, that they may obey thy holy Church, and observe all her precepts, and grow in grace and in every good work daily, to the greater glory of thy Name. Amen.

Our Father. Hail Mary.

SECOND PRAYER, FOR THE ROOTING OUT OF HERESIES

O MOST pitiful Lord Jesus Christ, true Light for the enlightening of the Gentiles, we beseech thy clemency that thou wouldst regard the destruction of so many souls, which through the cunning of the ancient serpent and the wiles of heretics have been plunged in deep and utter darkness. Can it be, O most merciful Jesus, that thou shouldst suffer those helpless souls, which thou hast redeemed with thy own precious Blood, to be deceived by the devil and subject to his sway? Canst thou permit so many wretched souls to be daily thrust down to hell for lack of the true faith? Remember O Christ Jesus, how many toilsome journeys thou didst undertake for their salvation, and what grievous stripes and wounds thou didst receive for their redemption. We beseech thee, therefore, by the virtue of thy most bitter Passion and death, that thou wouldst vouchsafe to crush and extinguish those cursed heresies, and to convert the hearts of all hardened heretics to thy true faith. Amen.

Our Father. Hail Mary.

THIRD PRAYER, FOR CONCORD AMONGST CHRISTIAN PRINCES

O SWEETEST Jesus, who art the Author of unity and Lover of peace, we implore thy clemency, that thou wouldst vouchsafe to bestow upon all Christian princes peace and true concord, that so thy Church may evermore serve thee with peaceful and undistracted devotion. Remember, O pitiful Jesus, how much innocent blood is continually shed by the scourge and storm of war. See how many are hurled down into extremest distress of body and mind. O most loving Jesus, who hast ever so supremely loved peace, and didst so often speak peace to thy disciples, we beseech thee by the ineffable love of thy Heart that thou wouldst deign to grant thy peace to all Christian kings and princes, and to bind them together in the most perfect bond of charity and concord; so that thy people may be ruled and governed in quietness and peace, and strengthened and kept in thy holy service. Vouchsafe to grant us this grace for the sake of thine infinite goodness and mercy. Amen.

Our Father. Hail Mary.

For these intentions, you may say with advantage the Litany of the Saints, or the Rosary, &c.

PRAYER FOR A PRIEST BEFORE SAYING MASS

O THOU supreme and adorable Trinity, I, the greatest of sinners, whom thou hast nevertheless called by thy grace to the office of the priesthood, propose and intend to touch and handle these most sacred Mysteries and to offer to thee the unbloody sacrifice. Wherefore, in union with that infinite love wherewith thou hast so loved the world that thou didst give thine only-begotten Son; in union with that boundless charity wherewith the same thine only-begotten Son took to himself our nature, and instituted and commanded us to offer this sacrifice, and offered himself for us on the altar of the cross, and doth still unceasingly offer himself in the heavens by showing for us his sacred scars and wounds, our ever-loving, ever-faithful advocate with thee; in union with all the love, reverence, and devotion wherewith any of thy priests hath ever offered it. I will draw near to thy altar and offer this tremendous sacrifice, together with all which are now being offered to thee all over the world.

Wherefore, O most holy Father, I lay upon thine altar and offer to thee all the merits, virtues, and good works which thy only-begotten Son wrought during his whole life on earth, and especially his most holy Passion, cross, and death, his Humanity and his Divinity; and together with these I offer thee all the merits of the blessed Mary his Mother, and of all the saints, all the wounds and the throes of thy martyrs, all the mortifications and austerities of confessors, all the chaste love of virgins, all the tribulations and groanings of the afflicted, all the misery and the needs of the poor, and all the whole treasure of our holy Mother the Church. And to these I desire and intend to add whatever good words, or deeds, or thoughts I, or any of those with whom I am especially connected, have thought or said or done for thy glory, and all the sorrow and adversity we have ever endured for thy sake. Would that all our works were such as we might presume to offer and set forth before thee; but do thou condescend to receive them, even such as they are.

And all these good works and sufferings, thus united with this sacrifice, I offer thee, O most holy Father, through thine only-begotten Son, in the power of the Holy Ghost, in my own name, and in that of all my especial friends and of all thy holy Church, as our part of that supreme worship, adoration, and glory, which are due to thee the supreme Lord of all: in true and adequate thanksgiving for all the riches of thine inexhaustible goodness, which thou hast bestowed on the Sacred Humanity of our Lord Jesus Christ, on the ever-blessed Virgin Mary, and all the saints of heaven, and on all thy creatures throughout this thy world, and on me and my especial friends in our bodies and in our souls: in expiation and reparation of every insult and wrong ever done to thee by all sinners, of whom I am chief and worst: and finally, for that supreme good pleasure, that joy and delight, which thou dost ever receive from this most acceptable oblation.

Next, 1 offer it to thee for the especial and signal increase of joy and glory to the sacred Humanity of our Lord Jesus Christ, in memory and veneration of his most holy Incarnation, Nativity, Life, Passion, and Death, in memory and honour of all his sighs, his tears, his wounds, his sorrows, and of each drop of his most precious Blood poured out for us; and for the special increase of bliss to the ever-blessed Virgin Mary and all the saints, especially N.

Thirdly, I offer it to thee for our holy Mother the Church, and for all her members and children; beseeching thee through the infinite merits of this sacrifice that thou wouldst vouchsafe to keep and defend it, to extend it, and make it perfect in every good work; in satisfaction, also, and in expiation of all the sins of all the whole world, and especially of those which I, alas, or any of my especial friends have ever committed against thee.

Lastly, I offer it to thee with all the energy of my whole being for myself, most unworthy of thy servants, and for my parents, brothers, sisters, relations, and benefactors; for all who are sick or afflicted, or in any need or tribulation, and for all for whom thy beloved Son immolated himself, and still longs to immolate himself yet again; and for all who are detained in purgatory, especially N., for whom thou knowest I am especially bound to pray.

Behold, O my Lord, since thou hast willed me to perform the office of a priest, I now discharge my ministry and office with thee for all these; these all wait for the lifting up of my weak hands, for the oblation of this availing sacrifice. For all these I will draw near now to thine altar, bearing my own miseries and iniquities and the iniquities and miseries of all these; and I will now offer them to thee in the spirit of humility and with a contrite heart, and spread them all forth before thy face, that by the virtue of this sacrifice all our sins may be blotted out and all our miseries relieved.

But, O Lord, how shall I intercede for the sins of others, who am not secure by reason of my own? How shall I implore thy mercy for others, who have rendered myself unworthy of the least grace or mercy at thy hands, by the reckless waste I have made of my whole life and by my wretched conduct towards thee? Wherefore in the bitterness of thy Passion I pour out my complaint before thee, bemoaning and bewailing everything whereby I have hindered the action of thy grace and quenched thy Spirit within me, and offended thee by my multiplied sins and negligences. For all these let the groanings of my heart come up before thee, and receive the wailing cry of repentance which I address towards thee because of my wretchedness and my wickednesses. O most compassionate Jesus, blot out all my sins; I do most heartily grieve for them; blot them all out with that love wherewith thou hast washed away the sins of the whole world. Bedew my dry and parched soul with the tears thou didst shed, anoint it with the myrrh of the sorrow thou didst endure, cleanse it with thy most precious Blood which thou didst shed for me with such lavish prodigality. Put forth thy hand from above, strengthen me now, and render me worthy to celebrate aright this adorable sacrifice. May the Holy Ghost come upon me, and the power of the Most High overshadow me, that I may be enabled to stand before thy dread altar, without being swept from thy presence, and that I may touch and handle, and offer and immolate, the spotless Lamb of God with a pure heart and undefiled hands, to thine everlasting glory and to the salvation of all the whole world. Amen.

THE LAST WILL AND TESTAMENT
OF THE SOUL

FROM THE REVELATIONS OF ST. GERTRUDE AND
ST. MECHTILDE

This may be regarded as the quintessence and summary of all the prayers contained in this little book, and it is of great and tried efficacy in quelling the rage of the assaults of our enemies in the hour of our death; wherefore you will do well to repeat and renew it at least four times a year. When you are ill, you should read it over with great devotion, or have it read to you if you cannot read it yourself; and at the end of each clause you should say: This is verily and indeed my will and desire.

In the name of the most Holy Trinity. Amen.

INASMUCH as I, a most miserable sinner, am most certain that I shall die, but most uncertain of the hour of my death, therefore now, while I have the full use of all my powers and faculties, I will publish and declare before thee, O most blessed Trinity, and in presence of all the court of heaven, this my last will, how I wish to live and to die. And lest it should be in any way changed or made void, I draw up and write this my testament, beseeching thee that it may remain in full force throughout eternity. Do thou, therefore, O most holy Father, look now on me thy most unworthy servant with the eyes of thy compassion, even as thou didst look upon thine only-begotten Son in the Garden of Olives as he lay prostrate on the ground before thee, disposing and bequeathing all his merits for the benefit of his Church. And as thou didst receive the prayer of the same thy Son as an odour of well-pleasing fragrance, so do thou deign to hold this my last will as a reasonable service, ratified by that, and acceptable in thy sight.

First: in the clearest form and most binding manner I bequeath and make over wholly to thee, O most blessed Trinity, my body and my soul, and all the works which I have done with them throughout the whole course of my life. And I give thee highest and everlasting thanks that thou hast made me a rational creature, hast regenerated me in holy baptism, hast sanctified me with the other Sacraments of thy grace, and hast bestowed on me in body and in soul, in general and in particular, innumerable good gifts. Wherefore I acknowledge that thou alone hast rightful dominion over me, and that thou alone, and none other besides thee, art my supreme and sovereign Lord.

Secondly: I ascribe to thee alone, my Lord and my God, all the good, and all the graces and favours which I have ever received from thee, in body and in soul; and I acknowledge that of thine unfathomable goodness, and through the intercession of thy saints, thou hast bestowed on me a thousandfold more good than I have ever deserved at thy hands, and that thou hast provided for me both in body and in soul, in prosperity and in adversity, with such exquisite discrimination of my need, that no power, or wisdom, or goodness but thine could have so ordered my lot. Wherefore I will sing thy praises and offer thee my thanksgivings with all my powers throughout eternity.

Thirdly: I firmly believe and profess the true faith which I received in my baptism, and all and every one of the articles thereof, in such manner and form as the one holy Catholic Church believes and professes them, and I am most ready rather to pour out my life and my blood than to deny one article of that true faith. And if through the craft and subtilty of the enemy of my soul, there should be in me at my last hour one thought, word, or action, which does not fully accord with this sacred faith, I hereby declare such thought, word, or action to be void and of no effect. And lest this should be the case, I commend my faith to thy omnipotence, thy wisdom, and thy goodness, O my God, that in the hour of my death it may be found whole and intact.

Fourthly: I detest and abhor all and every one of the sins which I have committed from my youth to this hour, of whatever kind they may be, and however committed; and I most bitterly and vehemently grieve for them, O most compassionate God, simply and purely for love of thee, and I most earnestly desire that this my sorrow were a thousand-fold more bitter and more vehement. And in supply of all that is lacking to my sorrow, I offer thee that contrition which thy only-begotten Son felt for the sins of the whole world. And that I may, at least in some degree, satisfy thee for the most grievous wrongs I have done thee, I offer myself to thee, protesting my readiness to suffer most willingly and gladly whatever vengeance thou mayest be pleased to exact from me.

Fifthly: and whereas all my satisfaction falls infinitely short of my debt to thee, I betake myself to the most abundant treasury of the merits of Jesus Christ; and I offer thee all the long Passion he endured from the first moment of his Conception until he bowed his head upon the cross and gave up the ghost. Moreover, I plunge and hide all my sins and negligences in his most sacred Wounds; beseeching thee that thou wouldst vouchsafe to wash away all my stains in his most precious Blood, and to inflame me with the fire of his love.

Sixthly: I most humbly ask pardon of all and every one whom I have ever grieved or offended by word or deed, and I declare myself ready to make full amends with my own person, according to the measures of thy most exact justice, for all the loss I have occasioned them in their honour or in their substance. And I do from my heart pardon and forgive every injury, insult, or wrong whereby any person has offended me by word or deed, even as our Lord Jesus Christ, while hanging upon the cross, forgave his enemies and murderers, and prayed for them to his Father.

Seventhly: I acknowledge and profess that I could not hope to attain heaven by my own merits; wherefore I put not my trust in them, but only in the merits and passion of thy beloved Son, and in the patronage and intercession of thy Saints. And in these I so firmly place my trust, that I cannot even conceive that I can perish everlastingly, yea, though I had offended thee a thousand times more than I have done; for I know that thy mercy is infinitely above my sins, and that the passion of thine only Son is of immeasurably greater weight in the balance of thy justice.

Eighthly: I wholly commit and resign to thy most holy will myself, and all that I am, or have, or can do, deliberately choosing and imploring of thee that that will may be most fully and entirely done in me, by me, and in all that concerns me. I do not desire to live one hour longer than it pleases thee. I do not desire to depart hence by this or that kind of death or sickness, but purely and alone by that which thou shalt appoint for me. Yea, were I now free to live on a thousand years amidst all imaginable delights, I would rather choose to die this moment, were it thy will, than to live one single moment longer than thou willest.

Ninthly: I love thee, O my God and my Love, and I desire to love thee for ever; for by reason of thy sovereign perfection and magnificence thou art most worthy of my love; and I would I could love thee a thousand-fold more than I do. Had I the capacity of the hearts of all men and all angels, I would most gladly employ all in thy love alone. But since I cannot love thee as I ought, I beseech thee that thou wouldst love thyself for me with a love worthy of thee.

Lastly: I profess that I desire to die as a true Catholic, and to partake of the most holy Sacraments of Penance, of Communion, and of Extreme Unction. I desire, moreover, to have my part and portion in all the Masses, prayers, and suffrages which shall be offered for the faithful departed henceforward until the day of judgment. Yea, were it in my power, I would ordain that upon every altar and by every priest the holy sacrifice of the Mass should be offered for me after my death to the end of time. But since this cannot be, I beseech thee, O Christ Jesus, that thou wouldst offer thyself for me to thy Father, a holocaust and a perpetual sacrifice for my innumerable sins. Moreover, I implore thee to send forth for the succour of my soul in its last agony but one of those sighs which burst forth from thy Heart in thine exceeding sorrow amidst the horrors of thine own agony, and to sprinkle upon it for its salvation one single drop of thy most precious Blood. Amen.

SEALING OF THE TESTAMENT

WHEREFORE, O most blessed Trinity, I now profess and declare before thee and all the court of heaven that all and every thing contained in this testament is my last sincere will and intention, in accordance with which I desire to live and to die. And I desire that this my testament be never in any wise evaded or made void, but that it may have its full force and effect before my death, and at my death, and after my death. And in case it should ever occur to me to revoke it, I now hereby declare that such revocation is to be held null and void.

I beseech thee then, O most tender Jesus, that thou wouldst deign to register this my last will publicly in the court of heaven, and to witness it with the signature of thy most holy Name, and to seal it with the impress of thy five sacred Wounds. And I beseech thee, O most blessed Virgin Mary, and thee, O blessed John the Evangelist, as though thou wert high chancellor of the everlasting kingdom, and thee also, O N. my beloved patron, who art assessor in that royal court of heaven, that ye would condescend to be the witnesses of this my last will, and to subscribe your names thereto, and to lay it up amongst the records of the most holy and adorable Trinity, so that it may be forthcoming to be presented to him at any time and in any emergency. And I resolve to keep always a copy thereof, signed with my own hand, so that it may be known to God and to all men whose I am in body and in soul, and in what manner I desire to live and to die.

And thus I a most unworthy servant of God, now sign and seal with my own hand.

N.

ADDITIONAL PRAYERS FOR MASS AND COMMUNION

From the Venerable Blosius

I ADORE thee, O glorious, bright, and ever-peaceful Trinity, Father, Son, and Holy Ghost, one God, my Hope, my Light, my Rest, my Joy, my Life, my All in all.

I give thee thanks, O Lord, that thou hast created me after thine own image, that thou hast borne with me all my life long to this day, notwithstanding my sins, with such long-suffering mercy, that thou hast rescued me from so many dangers, and encompassed me with innumerable blessings.

O compassionate Father, I offer thee the most holy Incarnation, Nativity, Life, Passion and Death, Resurrection and Ascension of thy only and well-beloved Son Jesus Christ in full expiation, propitiation, and satisfaction for all my sins and negligences, and also for the sins of all mankind. I offer thee all the toils, the afflictions, the outrages, the scorn, the blows and stripes, the woes and bitter anguish, wherewith he was overwhelmed. I offer thee the most precious Blood which he shed. I offer thee his humility, his patience, his charity, and his spotless innocence.

O Father, O Son, O Holy Ghost, my God who dwellest within me, grant me that I may be unable to think any thing, to will any thing, to speak any thing, to do any thing, but what is pleasing in thy sight. Grant that I and all men may ever do thy holy will. Make us well-pleasing to thee, and one with thee, so that thy delight may be to dwell in us. It is my bounden duty to praise thee, O Lord, and it is my most eager longing desire; but, inasmuch as I can never praise thee worthily, I implore thee that thou wouldst deign to offer to thyself most perfect praise within my heart, so that thou mayest sanctify for thyself, and accept as most grateful praise and adoration, every breath I draw, whether I wake or whether I sleep.

Glory be to the Father, &c.

From the same

I ADORE thee, I praise and magnify thee, O Jesus Christ, my Lord. I bless thee and give thanks to thee, thou Son of the living God, who, according to the will of the Father, and with the co-operation of the Holy Ghost, didst once vouchsafe to be conceived in the most chaste womb of the Blessed Virgin Mary and to be made man, partaker of my passible flesh and blood. O good Jesus, with what priceless and incomprehensible love hast thou loved me, that thou, the Lord of highest Majesty, shouldst condescend to empty thyself, taking the form of a servant! Thou, my God, art become my Brother! And what can I render thee for this thy compassion and thy tender mercy? Behold, I offer thee now my body and my soul for thine everlasting praise and glory.

I give thee thanks for thy most sacred Nativity, when thou didst come forth from the womb of the Virgin Mary, a tender Infant, in a stable, on a rough and bleak winter's night. Hail, thou sweetest Babe; hail, thou King of Glory, Light of the nations, Saviour so long desired, who didst not disdain to be wrapped for me in swaddling clothes, to be swathed with bands, to be laid on straw in a manger, and to draw thy sustenance from the Virgin's breast.

I give thee thanks for thy painful Circumcision, for thy Manifestation to the Gentiles and the bright star with which thou didst bring them to thy feet, for thy Presentation in the Temple, for the Flight into Egypt, and for all the privations and sufferings thou didst endure in thy most holy infancy, thy boyhood, and thy youth.

I give thee thanks for the sacred and worshipful Baptism which thou, the Creator of heaven and of earth, didst so humbly receive from thy servant John, for the Fast of forty days and forty nights wherewith thou wast afflicted and exhausted in the wilderness, and for all the foul temptations wherewith thou didst not refuse to be assailed by the devil.

I give thee thanks for thy saving doctrine, for the miracles thou didst work and the benefits thou didst bestow on the world, for thy journeyings, thy labour, and thy sorrows, for the hunger and the thirst, the cold and the heat thou didst endure, and for the manifold persecutions wherewith thou didst deign to be harassed for my salvation.

I give thee thanks for that marvellous condescension wherewith thou, their meek and lowly Master, didst kneel to wash thy disciples' feet and wipe them with a napkin.

I give thee thanks for the institution of the adorable Sacrament of the eucharist, in which, with most amazing liberality and unutterable love thou hast given and bequeathed thyself to us. Amen.

Glory be to the Father, &c.

DEVOTIONS BEFORE COMMUNION

From St. Ambrose

O COMPASSIONATE Lord Jesus Christ, I a sinner, nothing performing to my own merits, but trusting in thy mercy and goodness, draw near with awe and trembling to the table of thy sweetest banquet. For my heart and my body are stained with many sins, my mind and my tongue have not been kept with fitting diligence and circumspection. Wherefore, O compassionate Godhead, O dread and awful Majesty, I thy wretched creature, who am fallen into a great strait, betake myself to thee the Fountain of mercy; to thee I hasten that I may be healed; beneath thy protection I make my refuge; I long to have thee for my Saviour before whom I can in no wise stand as my Judge. To thee, O Lord, I now show my wounds; before thee I lay bare all this my shame. I know my sins, so many and so great, by reason of which I am afraid. I hope in thy mercies, which are past numbering. Look on me with the eyes of thy mercy, O Lord Jesus Christ, everlasting King, God and man, who wast crucified for man. Graciously hear me who hope in thee; have mercy on me who am full of miseries and of sins, O thou full and everflowing Fountain of pity and of mercy. Hail, thou saving Victim, offered for me and all mankind upon the tree of the cross. Hail, thou noble and precious Blood, which dost ever flow forth from the wounds of my crucified Lord Jesus Christ, and wash away the sins of the whole world. Remember thy creature, O Lord, whom thou hast redeemed with thine own Blood. I grieve that I have sinned; I do earnestly desire to amend what I have done amiss. Wherefore, O most merciful Father, take away from me all my iniquities and my sins, that, being cleansed in soul and in body, I may worthily receive the holy Food of the holy; and grant that the sacred taste of thy Body and Blood which I unworthy am about to receive may be to me the remission of my sins, the perfect expiation and cleansing of all my faults, the putting to flight of evil thoughts, the quickening and renewal of all good feelings, the healthful energy of all good works, the most assured protection of my body and soul from all the snares of my enemies. Amen.

From St. Thomas Aquinas

O ALMIGHTY, everlasting God, behold, I draw near to the Sacrament of thine only-begotten Son our Lord Jesus Christ; I draw near as a sick man to the Physician of life, as one defiled to the Fountain of mercy, as one blind to the Light of the eternal splendour, as one poor and needy to the Lord of heaven and earth. Wherefore, I implore the fulness of thine infinite bounty that thou wouldst vouchsafe to heal all my sickness, to wash away my defilement, to give light to my blindness, to enrich my poverty, and to clothe my nakedness, so that I may receive the Bread of Angels, the King of kings and Lord of lords, with such contrition and devotion, such purity and faith, such purpose and intention, as may avail to the welfare and salvation of my soul. Grant me, I beseech thee, to receive not only the Sacrament of the Body and Blood of my Lord, but also the very Reality and Substance of the Sacrament. O most gracious God, grant me so to receive the Body of thine only-begotten Son our Lord Jesus Christ, that very Body which he took of the Virgin Mary, that I may be truly incorporated into his mystical Body and so numbered amongst its members.

O most loving Father, grant me at last to behold with open face and for evermore the same thy beloved Son whom I purpose to receive now in my pilgrimage beneath the veils of the Sacrament. Who liveth and reigneth, &c.

PARAPHRASE OF THE LORD'S PRAYER, IN PREPARATION FOR HOLY COMMUNION

From the " Caeleste Palmetum "

O*UR Father,* most mighty, most wise, and most merciful, who, that thou mightest show to thy children thine exceeding sweetness, dost fill them in their hunger with thy sweetest Bread sent down from heaven, and dost in so fatherly and wonderful a manner sustain, cherish, and preserve all that thou hast created: behold I, who though most vile and unworthy am still one of thy children, now lift my eyes with confidence unto thee, *who art in heaven,* that thou mayest look down with the eyes of thy fatherly kindness on me, most wretched and needy, far away from my Father's face, a dweller amongst the children of Eve, in this vale of tears, a sojourner and an exile on earth, sighing with yearning desire towards thee, my most tender Father.

Hallowed be thy Name; for this is my chief desire and all the longing of my heart, that all I think, or speak, or do, may tend to the greater glory of thy holy Name; and now especially, when I am about to draw near to the sacred Mysteries of the Body and Blood of thy Son, I purpose this one thing only, this alone do I desire, that thy supreme majesty, power, goodness, and wisdom, may be truly and adequately praised and glorified; for to thee alone doth every creature owe all honour and glory, praise and thanksgiving for evermore, for that thou hast so loved us, that thou hast given thine only-begotten Son to be our Food, and the price of our salvation. And inasmuch as we cannot worthily praise thee for this thy great love, may the same thy Son glorify thee; for thou hast exalted him high over all, and hast given him a name which is above every name.

Thy kingdom come. In this Sacrament thou dost give us a foretaste of the blessedness and the entrancing delights of this thy kingdom. For as an earnest and pledge of our future glory, thou hast given us the Body and Blood of thy Son, and hast thus made us, by the grace of adoption, heirs of thyself, and fellow-heirs with thy Christ. Meanwhile, while we yet wander in the land of exile from the Lord, grant us so to use this sacred pledge that the kingdom of thy grace may daily advance in us more and more, and that the kingdom of thy glory may at length come in us.

Thy will be done. And what else is thy will but our sanctification, especially now that we are about to draw near to this most holy Sacra-

ment? Thou dost will that we should eat the
Flesh of the Son of Man and drink his Blood,
seeing that we cannot otherwise have life in
us. But who that knoweth his own weakness
and sickness could presume to do this, hadst
thou not with thy Son so lovingly and so
condescendingly willed and commanded it?
For the will of thy Son is one with thy will,
and his power one with thine. Wherefore since
thou dost will it thus, be that done which thou
willest, and as thou willest. And truly thou
dost will us to be holy, seeing that thy Son,
to whom we are about to draw near, is holy,
yea the Holy of holies. But who can make
us holy, save thee alone? Give, then, what
thou dost command; grant that we may not
handle holy things but holily, and with religious awe; wherefore, *as in heaven* thy saints
feed to the full on this living Bread in its very
reality, with pure hearts and glowing desire,
so may we *on earth* eat it, wrapped and veiled
beneath the sacramental species, with great
desire and pure affection, until, together with
thine elect, we feast on it, in its true form
and very substance, and are satisfied with the
fulness of thine house.

Give us this day our daily bread. The eyes
of all hope in thee, O Lord; and thou givest
them meat in due season. Thou openest thy
hand, and fillest with blessing every living
creature; and canst thou suffer me to want?
Thou knowest, O Lord, that the soul needs,

no less than the body, to be restored and sustained with food that it may live. For as our natural activity wears the body, so does the fierce heat of concupiscence wear and waste away the soul. But O, how blessed are thy children, who in the house of so great a Father, in thy holy Church, so abound with bread! Herein the bread of grace and of the word of God is most abundantly broken. Here is set forth for all the bread of the Sacraments, and above all that living Bread which came down from heaven, which was born in Bethlehem, the house of Bread, Bread of angels, Manna of heaven. O costly and noble Food! O unutterable love and mercy of the eternal Father! For to me who sow not, nor reap, nor gather into any garner, is given the Crown of the elect, and the Bread of Life from heaven. Thou, O Lord, didst sow it on the earth; thou didst reap it with the sickle of death; thou hast laid it up in the granary of thy Church, and dost give it all forth for the nourishment of thy children.

Grant me, then, O most tender Father, that I may be often and duly strengthened and refreshed with this Bread; may I daily receive thereof for my daily need, if not sacramentally, yet at least spiritually; for since I sin and fail day by day, so is it reasonable and just that I should day by day receive that which may recruit my wasted strength. Oh, that I may be so strengthened in this wilderness with this heavenly Bread and Viaticum, that in the strength of that food I may walk even unto the mount of God!

And forgive us our trespasses. Alas, how manifold and how grievous are our trespasses! For in many things we all offend, and in our misery and our poverty we have not wherewithal to acquit our great debt. But behold, O Lord, with thee there is mercy, and plenteous redemption with thy Son, whom, in pity of our misery, thou hast given to us. He is just and undefiled and free from all sin, and he hath paid our debt; he hath expiated our sins; he hath made abundant satisfaction to thy justice, in that he hath given to us the inexhaustible treasure of his merits and the infinite worth of his Blood.

And all this treasure and this worth we have laid up for us and hidden in this most precious Sacrament. Wherefore, O eternal Father, I offer thee now this treasure that thou mayest take thence whatever thou dost require of me for my manifold debts. I have not wherewith to pay thee, but the merits of thy Son abound to overflowing, that therefrom all our debts may be for ever discharged. For his sake, then, forgive us, even as we forgive all that trespass against us; as we forgive, lest we be without that perfect bond of charity, and so unworthily touch the Sacrament of peace and oneness; lest we should seek in vain unto God for forgiveness if we keep anger against our fellow-men. For what part or communion can we have in the Body and Blood of the Lord, if we are not united in communion of peace and love with the members of his mystical Body, that is, with all around us?

Wherefore it behoveth us, when we desire to draw near to the altar, first to be reconciled with our brethren, if they have anything against us, and so to come and offer unto thee our gift. This thy Son both taught us to do, and did for our example. For whilst hanging upon the cross and paying the debts of all men, he forgave all his enemies, and prayed meekly to thee for his tormentors, saying: Father, forgive them. Forgive me, therefore, all my trespasses, for which thy Son offers thee evermore all his merits; for, apart from these merits, if thou, O Lord, wilt mark iniquities, Lord, who shall stand it?

And lead us not into temptation. O Lord, who hast prepared before us a table against all who trouble us, and settest forth thereon the Bread which strengtheneth man's heart against all the temptations of the world, the flesh, and the devil, grant me through this heavenly and life-giving food strength and courage, that I may never yield in the hour of temptation, but may steadfastly cleave to thee.

May I not seek the friendship of this world, nor be conformed to its spirit, but may I be so transformed by the virtue of this heavenly food that I may desire to please thee alone, and fear nothing but to displease thee. May the earth grow vile in my eyes while I here behold the heavens, and embrace within me the Lord of the whole earth. May the pleasures of the flesh cease to attract me, seeing that it is given me to feed upon the Flesh of the Lamb without spot and on the Manna of heaven, in which I find pleasures greater far, and all conceivable sweetness of delight. And wherein shall the devil prevail against me when my God himself is with me? For if God be for us, who is against us?

But deliver us from evil. For in this life we stand exposed to many miseries and woes, and these are evils in so far as they cast us down who are so weak, and withdraw us from thee; for to be separated from thee, the one supreme and only Good, is in truth the greatest and worst of evils. And who shall deliver us from this evil but thou alone the Source of all good, and Jesus Christ, whom thou hast given us to be our advocate with thee, and the author of all salvation and blessedness, who hath delivered us from sin and death with his own Blood.

Grant now unto us through his mediation that all things may work together to us for good, for there is salvation for us in none other. Wherefore, as he is truly present in this Sacrament, so may he be with us every where and ever more; may he feed us, rule us, preserve us, protect us, lead us according to his good and loving will as the sheep of his pasture; whatever shall befall us will be no evil to us if it does not separate us from our chief Good, for it is good for me to adhere to my God. For what have I in heaven but thee? and besides thee what do I desire upon earth?

DEVOTIONS AFTER COMMUNION

1. *From St. Thomas Aquinas*

I GIVE thee thanks, O holy Lord, Father almighty, eternal God, that thou hast vouchsafed, for no merit of my own, but of the mere condescension of thy mercy, to satisfy me a sinner and thine unworthy servant with the precious Body and Blood of thy Son our Lord Jesus Christ. I implore thee, let not this holy communion be to me an increase of guilt unto my punishment, but an availing plea unto pardon and forgiveness. Let it be to me the armour of faith and the shield of good will. Grant that it may work the extinction of my vices, the rooting out of concupiscence and lust, and the increase within me of charity and patience, of humility and obedience. Let it be my strong defence against the snares of all my enemies, visible and invisible; the stilling and the calming of all my impulses, carnal and spiritual; my indissoluble union with thee the one and true God, and a blessed consummation at my last end. And I beseech thee that thou wouldst vouchsafe to bring me, sinner as I am, to that ineffable banquet where thou, with the Son and the Holy Ghost, art to thy Saints true and unfailing Light, fulness of content, joy for evermore, gladness without alloy, consummate and everlasting bliss. Through the same, &c.

2. *From St. Bonaventura*

O SWEETEST Lord Jesus Christ, pierce, I beseech thee, the inmost marrow of my soul with the tender and life-giving wound of thy love, with true, and calm, and holy apostolical charity, so that my whole soul may ever languish and faint for love of thee, and for desire of thee alone. May it long for thee and pine for thee in the courts of thy house; may it desire to be dissolved and to be with thee. Grant that my soul may hunger for thee, thou Bread of angels, thou refreshment of holy souls, our daily supersubstantial Bread, having all manner of sweetness and savour, and all most thrilling delights. May my heart ever hunger for thee and feed on thee, on whom angels long to look; and may my inmost soul be filled with the sweetness of the taste of thee. May it ever thirst for thee, thou Well of life, thou Fountain of wisdom and knowledge, thou Source of everlasting light, thou torrent of pleasures, thou fatness and abundance of the house of God; may it ever yearn towards thee, seek thee, find thee, tend towards thee, attain to thee, meditate ever on thee, speak of thee, and work all things to the praise and glory of thy Name, with humility and discretion, with love and delight, with ready care and glad affection, with perseverance even unto the end; and do thou be alone and evermore my hope, my whole trust, my riches, my delight, my gladness and my joy, my rest and my calm repose, my peace and my sweet content, my fragrance and my sweetness, my food and my refreshment, my refuge and my help, my wisdom, my portion, my own possession and my treasure, in whom my mind and my heart are fixed and rooted firmly and immovably for evermore. Amen.

3.

I HUMBLY implore thine ineffable mercy, O my Lord Jesus Christ, that this Sacrament of thy Body and Blood, which I unworthy have now received, may be to me the cleansing of all my sins, the strengthening of what is weak within me, and my sure defence against all the perils of the world. May it bestow on me thy forgiveness and establish me in grace; may it be to me the medicine of life, the abiding memory of thy Passion, my stay in weakness, the Viaticum and sure supply of all my pilgrimage. May it lead me as I go, bring me back when I wander, receive me when I return, uphold me when I stumble, raise me again when I fall, strengthen me to persevere even unto the end, and bring me to thy glory. O most high God, may the blissful presence of thy Body and Blood so change the taste of my heart, that it may find no sweetness more in aught besides thee alone, may love no other beauty, seek no unpermitted love, desire no consolation, admit no other delight, care for no honour but thine, stand in fear of no enemy or suffering. Who livest and reignest, &c.

PIOUS ASPIRATIONS TO JESUS

I HAVE found him whom my soul loveth; I hold him, and will not let him go. I embrace thee, O my Jesus, and receive the full joy of my love. I possess thee, thou treasure of my heart, in whom I possess all things. I implore thee, let my soul feel the power of thy presence; let it taste how sweet thou art, O my Lord, that, led captive by thy love, it may seek none else besides thee, nor love any else but for thy sake. Thou art my King; forget not my tribulation and my need. Thou art my Judge; spare me, and be merciful to my sins. Thou art my Physician; heal all my infirmities. Thou art the Spouse of my soul; betroth me to thyself for evermore. Thou art my Leader and my Defender, place me by thy side, and then I care not who lifteth his hand against me. Thou hast offered thyself a Victim for me, and I will sacrifice to thee a sacrifice of praise. Thou art my Redeemer; redeem my soul from the power of hell, and preserve me. Thou art my God and my All; for what have I in heaven but thee, and besides thee what do I desire upon earth? Thou, O my God, art the God of my heart, and my portion for ever. Amen.

PARAPHRASE OF THE "ANIMA CHRISTI"

From the "Caeleste Palmetum"

SOUL of Christ, sanctify me.
Body of Christ, save me.
Blood of Christ, inebriate me.
Water out of the Side of Christ, wash me.
Passion of Christ, strengthen me.
O good Jesus, hear me;
Hide me within thy Wounds;
Suffer me not to be separated from thee.
Defend me from the malignant enemy,
Call me at the hour of my death,
And bid me come unto thee,
That with thy Saints I may praise thee
For all eternity. Amen.

Soul of Christ, adorned with all the greatest graces and gifts of the Holy Ghost, *sanctify me* by a lively faith, a steadfast hope, a perfect charity, which neither tribulations nor anguish, nor even death itself can shake or weaken. O *Soul,* which art the soul of Christ by natural indwelling in his sacred Body, be thou likewise mine by thy gracious aid and working within me, and *sanctify me* with pious thoughts and holy affections. Be thou the soul and the life of my soul; for without thee all our life is but death.

Body of Christ, given for us not only to most bitter death, but for the life-giving Good of our soul, and the remedy of immortality, and an everabiding Sacrifice, *save me.* O divine Head, wherein are all the treasures of the wisdom and knowledge of God, rule and direct me. O most mild and benignant Eyes, so often dimmed with tears for me, look down upon me. O Tongue of my Saviour, which hast the words of everlasting life, teach me. O most mighty Hands, at whose touch diseases fled, and the blind saw, and the dead were raised, take away all the languors and the diseases of my soul and my body, scatter my darkness, and restore to me the life of grace. O Feet of Jesus, so beautiful, bringing salvation to the whole world, would that with Magdalene I might embrace you and kiss thee, and so find pardon of all my sins! O Breast most lovely, shrine of the Godhead, altar of love, unite my heart to thine, and enkindle it with thy love. So to me to live will be Christ, and to die will be gain.

Blood of Christ, poured out for love of me, inebriate me, that I may strive to give thee back love for love, to suffer death for death, and ever to resist all sin steadfastly and generously even unto blood.

Water out of the Side of Christ, flowing from his riven Heart, *wash me.* More and yet more wash me, and cleanse me from my sin, that through that pierced side I may be admitted to embrace his sacred Heart.

Passion of Christ, strong and mighty Passion, which bore the whole burden of our sins, *strengthen me;* fortify me against all adversities; impart to me courage to endure with strong and glad heart all contumely and insult for the sake of my Lord Jesus Christ.

O good Jesus, Fountain and Spring of all goodness, *hear me,* exceeding sinner though I be; for thy tenderness and thy mercy still receiveth sinners. Open wide the bowels of thy loving mercy, and *hide me within thy Wounds,* which thou hast appointed to be the refuge and shelter of the wretched; let me not become a prey to my enemies, nor fall into the hands of my justly offended God. Here will I dwell securely hidden; and here, O good Jesus, will I sing of thy loving-kindnesses for ever.

Suffer me not, in anger at the multitude and the heinousness of my sins, *to be separated from thee.* This I implore of thee by thy most sacred Wounds, by thy most precious Blood, by thy most bitter Passion and Death. For were I separated from thee mine enemies would say: God hath forsaken him, follow after and take him, for there is none to deliver. Wherefore again and again I cry to thee, O my Jesus;

suffer me not to be separated from thee for ever.

Defend and protect *me from the malignant enemy*, who ever goeth about as a roaring lion, seeking whom he may devour; lest my enemy say: I have prevailed against him.

In the hour of my death, when I am forsaken by all creatures, when I must go forth trembling from this changing world into my eternal home and dwelling-place, *call me*, thy lost and strayed sheep, who have so often refused to hear thy voice, *Call me*, though unworthy to be called a sheep of thy fold, for all thy sheep know and hear thy voice. Yet *call me* still, not for my merits, but in thine own tender mercy; for what profit is there in my blood if I go down into destruction!

And *bid me come to thee*, my supreme and only Good, to enjoy whom I was created, bid me come to thee, who callest all to thee, and who alone dost suffice unto me. For what have I in heaven but thee, and besides thee what do I desire upon earth, since thou, O my God, art the God of my heart, and my portion for ever?

That with thy saints, all unworthy though I be to be received into their fellowship, yet admitted therein of thy boundless goodness, *I may praise thee*, my God and my Saviour, *for all eternity. Amen.* Oh, when, my Jesus, shall I come and appear before thy face?

PRAYER OF ST. THOMAS AQUINAS, FOR ALL
VIRTUES NEEDFUL TO A CHRISTIAN MAN

O MERCIFUL God, grant that I may eagerly desire, carefully search out, truthfully acknowledge, and ever perfectly fulfil all things which are pleasing unto thee. Order all my state for the glory and honour of thy Name alone; and grant me to know what thou dost require me to do, and give me to do it as is fitting, and profitable to my salvation. Grant that I may not fail or swerve either in prosperity or in adversity; that I be not lifted up by the one, nor cast down by the other. Let me joy in nothing but what leads to thee, nor grieve for anything but what leads away from thee; let me neither seek to please, nor fear to displease, any but thee alone. May all transitory things grow vile in my eyes, O Lord, and may all that is thine be dear to me for thy sake, and thou, O my God, dear above them all. May all joy be irksome to me that is without thee, nor may I desire anything that is apart from thee. May all labour and toil delight me which is for thee, and all rest be weariness which is not in thee. Grant me, O Lord, continually to lift up my heart towards thee, and to bring sorrowfully to my mind my many short-comings, with full purpose of amendment. Make me, O Lord, obedient without demur, poor without repining, chaste without stain, patient without murmur, humble without pretence, joyous without frivolity, fearful without abjectness, truthful without disguise, given to good works without presumption, faithful to rebuke my neighbour without arrogance, and ever careful to edify him both by word and example without pretension. Give me, O Lord God, an ever-watchful heart, which no subtle speculation may lure from thee; a noble heart, which no unworthy affection can draw downwards to the earth; an upright heart, which no insincere intention can warp aside; an unconquerable heart, which no tribulation can crush or quell; a free heart, which no perverted or impetuous affection can claim for its own. Bestow on me, O Lord my God, understanding to know thee, diligence to seek thee, wisdom to find thee, a life and conversation which may please thee, perseverance in waiting patiently for thee, and a hope which may embrace thee at the last. Grant me to be pierced with compunction by thy sorrows through true repentance, to improve all thy gifts and benefits during this my pilgrimage through thy grace, and so at length to enter into thy full and consummate joy in thy glory. Through our Lord Jesus Christ thy Son, who liveth and reigneth, &c.

PRAYER BEFORE STUDY

From St. Thomas Aquinas

O INEFFABLE Creator, my Lord and my God, who in unsearchable wisdom hast formed the nine choirs of angels, and set them on high above the heavens in a wonderful order, and hast exquisitely fashioned and knit together all the parts of the universe; do thou, who art the true Fountain and one essential Principle of light and wisdom, deign to shed the brightness of thy light upon the darkness of my understanding, and thus to disperse the twofold darkness, of sin and of ignorance, wherein I was born. O thou who makest eloquent the tongues of babes, instruct my tongue, and pour forth on my lips the grace of thy blessing. Grant me acuteness in understanding what I read, power to retain it, subtilty to discern its true meaning, readiness in learning, and clearness and ease in expressing it. Do thou order my beginnings, direct and further my progress, complete and bless my ending; through Christ our Lord.

FOR THE CONVERSION OF THE HEATHEN

From St. Francis Xavier

O ETERNAL God, Creator of all things, remember that the souls of unbelievers, heretics, and sinners were made by thee, and fashioned to thy own image and likeness. Behold, O Lord, how many of them go down into hell, to the dishonour of thy holy Name. Remember that thy beloved Son Jesus hath suffered a most cruel death for their salvation. Suffer not, I beseech thee, O Lord, thy Son to be any longer despised by unbelievers, heretics, and sinners; but graciously hear the prayers of holy men and of all the Church, the most holy spouse of thy Son; remember thy mercies and thy compassions; remember no more their idolatry, their unbelief, their hardness of heart, nor their evil will; but give them grace at length to know, to fear, and to love him whom thou hast sent, Jesus Christ our Lord, who is our salvation, our life and resurrection, through whom we are saved and made free, to whom be all glory for evermore. Amen.

FOR A HAPPY DEATH

O LORD Jesus Christ, Prince both of life and of death, whose we are in life and in death, I beseech thee by thy holy death for us upon the cross, that thy coming to me in death may not find me asleep, careless and unemployed, but watching and ready for thee. I beseech thee, let me not depart this life in impenitence, nor die an unprepared death; but strengthen and fortify me with the true Catholic faith, with sincere contrition, with a good confession and fitting satisfaction, and with the most holy Sacraments of the Eucharist and of Extreme Unction. Then, when all the vain and fleeting things of earth leave me, forsake me not, O thou who abidest ever with thy chosen; be with me in that last dread agony when my struggle with the enemy will be most deadly and decisive. May thy holy angels be with me then, and shield me from all temptations and give me consolation and fortitude amidst my sufferings. May faith and hope and charity and patience be strong within me. Enable me with unclouded consciousness to commend my soul into thy hands, and may I fall asleep in holy peace, and so pass in safety into the kingdom which thou hast purchased for us with so great a price. Remember me then, O Lord, as thou didst promise to remember the penitent thief at his last hour, and in thy mercy didst bestow on him what thou hadst promised. Amen.

THE LIFE EVERLASTING

From St. Augustine

AS the hart panteth after the fountain of waters, so my soul panteth after thee, O God. My soul hath thirsted after the strong living God; when shall I come and appear before the face of God? O thou Fountain of life, thou spring of living waters, when shall I pass from this desert, pathless, barren land to the waters of thy sweetness, to see thy beauty and thy glory, and to slake my soul's thirst at the gushing streams of thy love? I thirst, O Lord: thou art the Fountain of life; give thou me to drink. I thirst, O my Lord; I thirst for thee, the living God: oh, when shall I come and appear before thy face! Shall I in very deed see that day, that day of joy and gladness, that day which the Lord hath made that we may rejoice and be glad in it?

O bright and glorious day, which knoweth no evening, whose sun shall no more go down; in which I shall hear the voice of praise, the voice of joy and thanksgiving, thy voice saying unto me: Enter into the joy of thy Lord; enter into joy everlasting, into the house of the Lord thy God, where are things great and unsearchable, and wonderful things without number; enter into joy wherein is no sorrow, but untroubled gladness; wherein is all manner of good, and no manner of thing that is evil; where all thine heart's desire shall be satisfied, and all thou fearest and hatest shall be far from thee; where life shall be calm, and glad, and thrilling; wherein the hateful enemy shall not enter, nor any breath of temptation shall come near thee, where is supreme and settled security, and tranquil joy, and joyful happiness, and a happy eternity, an eternal blessedness, the blessed Trinity, and the unity of the Trinity, the Godhead in unity, the blissful vision of the Godhead: the joy of thy Lord!

O joy upon joy, joy transcending all joys! when shall I enter into thee, and behold my Lord, whose dwelling is in thee! I shall go thither and see this great sight. And now what keepeth me back? Woe is me, that my sojourning is prolonged! How long, O Lord, shall it be said to me: Wait, wait, yet awhile? Come, O Lord, delay no longer! Come, Lord

Jesus Christ, and visit us in peace; come and bring forth thy captives from their dungeon, that they may praise thee with a perfect heart! Come, thou desire of all nations, show thy face, and we shall be saved! Come, my light, my Redeemer, bring my soul out of prison, that it may give thanks to thy Name.

Blessed art they who have passed over the great and wide sea to the eternal shore, and are now blessed in their desired rest. Blessed are they who have escaped from all evils, and are secure of their unfading glory in thee, thou kingdom of blessedness! How long shall I be tossed about on the waves of this my mortal life, crying unto thee, O Lord God, while thou hearest me not? Hear me, O Lord, from this great and wide ocean, and bring me to the everlasting haven.

O everlasting kingdom, kingdom of endless ages, whereon rests the untroubled light and the peace of God, which passeth all understanding, where the souls of the saints are at rest, and everlasting joy is upon their heads, and sorrow and sighing have fled away! Oh, how glorious is the kingdom in which all thy saints reign with thee, O Lord, clothed with light as with a garment, and having on their heads a crown of precious stones! For there is infinite unfading joy, gladness without sorrow, health without a pang, life without toil, light without darkness, life without death; there the vigour of age knows no decay, and beauty withers not, nor doth love grow cold, nor joy wane away, for there we look evermore upon the face of the Lord God of hosts.

O Christ, our refuge and strength, thou hope of humankind, thou whose light shineth from afar upon the dark clouds which hang around us; behold, thy redeemed ones cry unto thee, thy banished ones whom thou hast redeemed with thine own most precious Blood. Hear us, O God our Saviour, thou who art the hope of all the ends of the earth and of those that are afar off on the wide sea. We are tossed about on the wild and raging waves in the dark night; and thou, standing on the everlasting shore, dost behold our sore peril: save us for thy Name's sake. Guide us amidst the shoals and quicksands which beset all our course, and so bring us in safety to the haven where we desire to be. Amen.

BEHOLD, O good and most sweet Jesus, I cast myself upon my knees in thy sight, and with all the fervour of my soul I pray and beseech thee to vouchsafe to impress upon my heart lively sentiments of faith, hope, and charity, with true sorrow for my sins, and a most firm purpose of amendment, while, with great affection and grief of soul, I ponder within myself and mentally contemplate thy Five Wounds, having before my eyes what thou didst say of thyself, O good Jesus, by the Prophet David: "They have pierced my hands and my feet; they have numbered all my bones."

49820493R00157

Made in the USA
Columbia, SC
27 January 2019